THE COMPLETE GUIDE TO

DESIGNING YOUR OWN HOME

THE COMPLETE GUIDE TO

DESIGNING YOUR OWN HOME

SCOTT T. BALLARD, A.I.A.

BETTERWAY BOOKS

CINCINNATI, OHIO

The Complete Guide to Designing Your Own Home. Copyright © 1995 by Scott T. Ballard. Printed and bound in the United States of America. All rights reserved. No part of this book may be reproduced in any form or by any electronic or mechanical means including information storage and retrieval systems without permission in writing from the publisher, except by a reviewer, who may quote brief passages in a review. Published by Betterway Books, an imprint of F&W Publications, Inc., 4700 East Galbraith Road, Cincinnati, Ohio, 45236. (800) 289-0963. First edition.

Other fine Betterway Books are available from your local bookstore or direct from the publisher.

06 05 04 03 02   9 8 7 6 5

Library of Congress Cataloging-in-Publication Data

Ballard, Scott T.
    The complete guide to designing your own home / Scott T. Ballard.
        p.   cm.
    Includes index.
    ISBN 1-55870-334-9
    1. Architecture, Domestic—Amateurs' manuals. I. Title.
II. Title: Designing your own home.
NA7115.B289   1995
728'.37—dc20   94-32578
                                                                        CIP

Edited by R. Adam Blake
Interior design by Brian Roeth
Cover design by Clare Finney and Angela Lennert Wilcox
Cover photo by D. Altman Fleischer Photography
House model by Cynthia Williams, Architect, Cincinnati, Ohio

METRIC CONVERSION CHART

TO CONVERT	TO	MULTIPLY BY
Inches	Centimeters	2.54
Centimeters	Inches	0.4
Feet	Centimeters	30.5
Centimeters	Feet	0.03
Yards	Meters	0.9
Meters	Yards	1.1
Sq. Inches	Sq. Centimeters	6.45
Sq. Centimeters	Sq. Inches	0.16
Sq. Feet	Sq. Meters	0.09
Sq. Meters	Sq. Feet	10.8
Sq. Yards	Sq. Meters	0.8
Sq. Meters	Sq. Yards	1.2
Pounds	Kilograms	0.45
Kilograms	Pounds	2.2
Ounces	Grams	28.4
Grams	Ounces	0.04

ABOUT THE AUTHOR

Scott Ballard is a graduate of the University of Texas at Austin and has been practicing architecture for over twenty years. He has designed both residential and commercial projects throughout the United States as well as in Saudi Arabia, Malaysia and Singapore. He is also the author of the book *How to Be Your Own Architect*. He currently resides in Houston.

DEDICATION

To my beautiful wife Virginia, for whom I do everything I do.

Table of Contents

Introduction

To build is a noble task.

It is as basic as shelter and as ambitious as art. It is the production of order from chaos. It is the creation of something unique and special from a pile of parts. It is the complex orchestration of diverse materials, systems and labor toward a unified whole. It is having it the way you want it and not the way it comes. It is enduring. It is expensive. It is difficult.

Children stack colorful plastic doodads on top of one another before they can walk. Pharaohs and kings reserve their places in history by the pyramids, castles and cities they construct. Almost everyone has visions of building his own small castle, but most people will have to satisfy this dream of immortality with the construction of a backyard deck and barbecue because designing and building your own home is an expense few of us can afford. But, if you are reading this book, it may be because you are one of the lucky individuals who is financially stable enough and has the personal courage to take on one of the most rewarding and challenging endeavors of your life. It will be tough, but it will be worth it.

Designing and building your house will be one of the biggest and most important decisions you will make in your lifetime. It is big financially because it is the largest investment most of us make in our lives. It is big emotionally because it is very personal, and the decisions are tough and compromising and will actually be cast in concrete. More importantly, those decisions will greatly impact how you live your life during your time in that house.

Because a house is a very expensive and complicated thing to create and because the few lucky people who get to attempt it can only do it once or twice in their lifetimes, they never quite get it down. So there is a whole army of highly skilled professionals and specialists—from bankers to architects to contractors—available to assist you in the various stages of the project.

An owner may use as much or as little of the services of these professionals as he or she sees fit, but, more than likely, every owner will require the services of each of these specialists to some degree. In the end they will save you money by improving the quality of your project and reducing the risk factor of your investment. This book will take you step-by-step through the whole process, from your initial decision to build through your final punch list. It will explain in detail what service each of these specialists provides and at what price, which parts you have to do yourself, which parts you might want to do yourself, and which parts you will probably want to contract out to the right professional.

Most of these professional services are negotiable in quantity and price. There are also alternative services available in many areas at reduced costs. Depending upon the size and budget of your project, one of these scaled-down services may be all you need.

All these services should be considered your tools. This book will help you understand what job each tool performs and how much each tool costs. It will help you to define your job and select the right tool for it at the best price. But most importantly, this book will help you understand the workings of the residential design and construction industry and keep you where you should be—in control of your project and your consultants.

CHAPTER 1
GETTING STARTED

Once you have decided that you would like to build your own home, the idea seems to return again and again like a challenge, sounding more interesting and daring with each visitation.

But, where do you begin the process? You could look in the yellow pages under "Architects," make an appointment with one whose name sounds good, open your checkbook, and let the architect guide you through the process.

However, if you are reading this book, you probably would like to educate yourself more about the whole business before you commit yourself and open the money valve. This is a wise approach in several ways:

1. You can and should do much of the front end work yourself, saving money on fees.

2. There are a wide variety of design services available. This book will inform you on the comparable costs of the different services, the level of service to expect from each, and how much can be negotiated.

3. If you are properly informed, you can select the right service for your project and get it for the best price.

4. When you have decided which service is the best for your purpose, you will know how to find proper candidates, how to interview them, and how to know which one is best for you.

Figure 1-1 gives a general idea of how the process should work beginning with your decision to build and ending with move-in. Each bubble represents a landmark event in its proper order of occurrence; some events must follow others, and some can coincide with others in the same time sequence.

ESTIMATING COSTS

If you have decided to build a house in a certain location, your first question might well be, "How much will it cost?" If you can't afford it, you can forget about it and start thinking about that bass boat you wanted to buy.

Basically, if your house is in a city, good investment notions say that it should be about the same size and should cost about the same amount per square foot as the other new homes in the neighborhood. If there are no other new homes in the area and you don't mind the role of real estate pioneer, you should give careful consideration to its real value in that location if you were to sell it upon completion. In fact, before your bank will approve your construction loan, your lot and plans will be appraised by a professional real estate appraiser specifically for this purpose, and the loan amount you can qualify for will be based on that appraisal.

You can do your own calculations to determine if the project you have in mind is feasible in the area. First, locate existing projects for sale in the area that are new or fairly new and similar in size to your own. A call to the listing realtor will tell you the asking price for the project and the air-conditioned square foot area of the house. Dividing

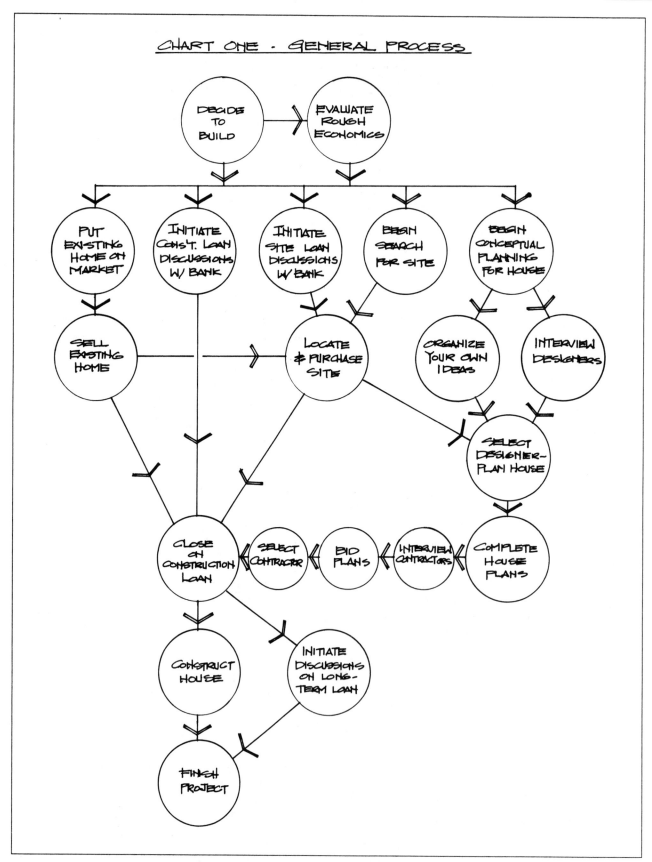

Figure 1-1: *Chart One—General Process*

the project cost by the house area will give you a cost per square foot for the whole project (including the lot cost).

(1.1) $\text{Project Sq. Ft. Cost} = \dfrac{\text{Total Project Cost}}{\text{Area of House}}$

The project square foot cost for your house should be comparable to the others you have checked out. Multiply the project square foot cost you have found by the area you would like to build. (Area is defined as the air-conditioned space of the house, not including garages, porches, terraces, balconies, attics, etc.) This will give you an idea of what your total project cost should be.

(1.2) $\text{Project Sq. Ft. Cost} \times \text{Area} = \text{Total Project Cost}$

This calculation also assumes that you will not "underbuild" or "overbuild" the neighborhood; that is, you will build a house of a similar size and quality to the other newer homes in the area.

To build too small or too inexpensive a house in a middle-class neighborhood would be just as problematic as building too large or too expensive a house in a poor neighborhood. It might suit your personal needs just fine, but few lending institutions will want to try to resell it if you die or otherwise default on the note, and therefore you will have a difficult time arranging the loan. Even if you can afford to build without borrowing, you should give serious thought to the resale risk in such situations.

If you are building in a new subdivision, there are usually minimum construction budgets required by the subdivision bylaws. If not, the above relationships still remain true.

If you are building in the country, the price becomes negotiable between you, your equity in the proposed project and your banker.

Construction Price

A more accurate approximation of the total project price can be found in the following way. First of all, break the total project cost down into its two component parts: construction price and lot price. Your construction price can be found by using Formula (1.3) (a variation of the above formulas) and selecting a square foot construction cost from Table One—Square Foot Costs (shown below)—with respect to the type and quality of construction you have in mind.

(1.3) $\text{Construction Price} = \text{Construction Cost} \times \text{Sq. Ft. Area}$

TABLE ONE—SQUARE FOOT COSTS

Type Construction and Improvements	Approximate Cost/Square Foot
Simple Wood Frame House Shingle roof Aluminum windows Carpet floors Wood siding	$50-$65/sq. ft.
Two Story Wood Frame House Shingle roof Aluminum windows Oak floors and carpet Brick veneer or stucco exterior	$70-$85/sq. ft.
Two Story Wood Frame House Tile roof Wood windows Oak, tile floors and carpet Brick veneer or stucco exterior Custom detailing	$85-$150/sq. ft. and up

The approximate area you will want to construct can be found in Table Two—House Area Ranges (shown on page 6).

A still more accurate way to estimate the area of your home is to write the design program for your project. This program is a list of all the rooms that you want with dimensions for each and the

TABLE TWO—HOUSE AREA RANGES

House Description	Approximate Area Range in Square Feet
2 BR, 1 Bath	1,000-1,500 sq. ft.
3 BR, 2 Bath	1,500-2,500 sq. ft.
4 BR, 2½ Bath	2,500-3,500 sq. ft.
4 BR, 3½ Bath	3,000 sq. ft. and up

corresponding area. The total area will then be multiplied by a factor to allow for the additional spaces that will flush out the plan, as shown in the following example.

Rooms	Dimensions	Area in Square Feet
Foyer	8' × 10'	80
Living Room	14' × 20'	280
Dining Room	14' × 17'	238
Family Room	20' × 20'	400
Breakfast Room	10' × 10'	100
Kitchen	13' × 18'	234
Powder Room	5' × 5'	25
Master BR	15' × 18'	270
Master Bath	7' × 15'	105
BR 2	12' × 14'	168
BR 3	12' × 14'	168
BR 4	12' × 14'	168
Bath 2	5' × 10'	50
Bath 3	5' × 10'	50
Utility Room	10' × 12'	120
Total Net Area		2,456 sq. ft.

This net area total is the area of the actual rooms themselves. It should be multiplied by a "gross area factor" to allow for miscellaneous support space such as circulation space between rooms, stairs and closets.

(1.4) Net Area × Gross Area Factor = Total Project Area

The gross area factor will vary from 1.2 (20 percent more area) to 1.4 (40 percent more area) for most houses depending upon the size of spaces such as the master closet and stairs and how efficiently the plan is designed.

Write your ideal design program and multiply the total net square footage by a gross area factor of 1.4 for your first calculation. Then compare that figure to the areas in Table Two (shown on the left), which are fairly tight but possible. Select a final area figure somewhere between the two for your budget calculation, depending upon how financially secure you feel at the moment.

Lot Price

Next, you can arrive at an approximate lot price by driving around and locating a lot for sale that is similar in location and size to the one you want. A phone call to the realtor will give you the asking price, and you should be able to assume a 10 percent discount for the actual selling price, including real estate brokerage fees. If the lot already has a house on it that must be removed, add another $5,000 to the price for demolition.

(1.5) Lot Price = Asking Price × 0.90 + 5,000 (demolition, if required)

Adding the above lot price to your project construction price will give you a good idea of your total project cost. To arrive at a grand total project cost, you should add another 10 percent to cover soft costs—the various associated fees such as design, engineering, loan points, construction loan interest, and a general contingency for extras and changes.

(1.6) Grand Total Project Cost = (Lot Price + Construction Price) × 1.10

FIGURING OUT WHAT YOU CAN AFFORD

This total price may seem like a lot of money, but you need only be concerned with whether or not you can qualify with the long-term lender for the monthly payment on the note.

First, it is necessary to determine what the actual note will be. Most lenders will require at least 10 percent and usually 20 percent down payment or owner equity in a house to reduce their risk in the project if the owner defaults. This equity will come from your savings or from the equity you have in your present home. In fact, any profit you derive from the sale of your present home must be reinvested in another home within twenty-four months (eighteen months for a used home), or you will be required to pay taxes on your profits. Therefore, it is usually a good idea to reinvest all the equity you take out of your present home into the new home just to escape the tax man. It will also greatly reduce your monthly payment.

Formula (1.7) calculates your total loan amount assuming a 20 percent equity.

(1.7) Loan Amount = Grand Total Project Cost $\times 0.80$

There is no way to guarantee what mortgage interest rates will be a year from now (the approximate time period between initiating the project and moving in), but we can usually assume they won't change too much from today's rates. Today's rates can be found in the business or real estate section of the Sunday paper. Using this rate, say 8.00 percent for 1994, you can use Table Three—Loan Amortization (shown at right)—to determine your monthly payment on your loan amount for both a fifteen-year and a thirty-year note.

This table shows the monthly payment required to amortize a loan of $1,000 for a fifteen- and thirty-year period. Use the following formula to find the total monthly payment required to amortize your loan.

(1.8) Monthly Payment $= \dfrac{\text{Dollar Figure From Table Three} \times \text{Loan Amount}}{1,000}$

After calculating your monthly amortization payment using the above formula, you must add an amount to cover property taxes and insurance on the house. If you have a home at present, you can locate the amount you pay for taxes and insurance and loan amortization from your payment booklet. If the budget for your new house is twice as much as the value of your existing home, you should double the amount you now pay in taxes and insurance

TABLE THREE—LOAN AMORTIZATION

Years of Loan	15	30
Percentage Rate	Monthly Payment For Each $1,000 Borrowed	
6.75	8.85	6.49
7.00	8.99	6.65
7.50	9.27	6.99
8.00	9.56	7.34
8.50	9.85	7.69
9.00	10.14	8.05
9.50	10.44	8.41
10.00	10.75	8.96
10.50	11.05	9.15
11.00	11.37	9.52
11.50	11.68	9.90
12.00	12.00	10.29
13.00	12.65	11.06

for the calculation of your new monthly payment. If your budget is only 25 percent more than the value of your existing home, add 25 percent more to your taxes and insurance premium, etc.

Now, simply add that amount for taxes and insurance to your monthly amortization payment to find your total monthly commitment on your new house.

An easier method is to use a multiplier factor of 1.3 to 1.4 (a 30 percent to 40 percent increase above your amortization payment) for taxes and insurance. That should be close to the correct amount in most urban areas. Use Formula (1.9) to approximate your total monthly payment.

(1.9) Total Monthly Payment = Amortization Payment $\times 1.35$

Loan and Mortgage Qualification

After calculating what your total monthly payment will be on your new home, you must determine if you can qualify for a loan of that amount. As I have already mentioned, the lender will not loan you the whole amount under any condition. In order to protect itself if it should have to take back the house, a lender will only finance 80 percent to 90 percent of the appraised value of the project—usually 80 percent. This means that you must come up with the first 20 percent out of savings or your equity in your existing home. If you can do this, move along to the next loan qualification hurdle.

Most lenders have a formula they use to qualify loan applicants for loan amounts. They usually will allow you to commit only 28 percent of your gross monthly income to cover your total house payment. Furthermore, your total fixed obligations (house payment, car payments, medical insurance, etc.) cannot exceed 36 percent of your gross monthly income.

Using the above figures, you can calculate the maximum amount of monthly payment for which you may qualify.

(1.10) Possible Monthly Payment = Gross Monthly
Income × 0.28

or inversely . . .

(1.11) $$\text{Monthly Gross Income Required for Certain Payment} = \frac{\text{Total Monthly Payment}}{0.28}$$

If you can qualify for more than the monthly payment required for your project, we can proceed through the book. If not, you may want to consider trimming your budget or the bass boat.

PROJECT COST AND LOAN QUALIFICATION

The following examples demonstrate how the previous discussions work—first from a project cost focus and second from a monthly payment qualifying focus. (Note: In the following calculations, numbers have been rounded off to the nearest dollar.)

Assumptions

The following information describes the house used in the examples.

Description of project: Two story, 3 BR, 2 bath, with family room, and 2 car garage

Materials: Brick veneer, composition shingle roof, wood floors downstairs, carpet upstairs, aluminum windows

Site: Infill lot in older neighborhood with existing house. Using formula (1.5):

Lot asking price	$150,000
Less 10 percent discount	−15,000
Actual sale price	$135,000
Plus demolition cost	+5,000
Total lot price	$140,000

Example One

Calculation One: Drive around the neighborhood and find the size and asking price for other new or similar projects in the area. Dividing those prices by the respective areas of the projects, we find that other projects are selling for approximately $120/square foot on the finished project (including land costs). According to Table Two (shown on page 6), a reasonable area for your project is around 3,000 square feet (with family room and breakfast room). Multiply your proposed area by the existing project square foot price. Using formula (1.2):

Existing project sq. ft. price	$120
Times proposed area	×3,000
Proposed total project cost	$360,000

Calculation Two: Using the above area and referring to Table One (shown on page 5), you decide on a square foot construction price of $70/square foot. Using formulas (1.3) and (1.6), find an approximate project price.

Total project area	3,000
Times cost/square foot	×$70
Total construction price	$210,000
Plus lot price (from above)	+140,000
Subtotal	$350,000
Plus 10% soft costs	+35,000
Grand total project cost	$385,000

Dividing this number by our proposed area yields the project square foot cost. Using formula (1.1):

$$\frac{\$385,000}{3,000} = \$128/\text{sq. ft.}$$

Comparing this project square foot cost to the existing projects for sale in the area shows approximately a 6 percent difference in existing market values and the cost of your new project. Therefore, you can feel reasonably sure that your project is feasible in the area and can be financed without excessive risk.

Calculation Three: For this calculation, list each major room you want in your house, the specific dimensions for each room, and the corresponding area for the room.

Rooms	Dimensions	Area in Square Feet
Foyer	8' × 8'	64
Living Room	15' × 20'	300
Dining Room	12' × 15'	180
Kitchen	8' × 15'	120
Breakfast Room	10' × 10'	100
Family Room	18' × 20'	360
Master BR	15' × 18'	270
Master Bath	7' × 12'	84
Bath 2	5' × 8'	40
BR 2	12' × 13'	156
BR 3	12' × 13'	156
Total Net Area		1,830 sq. ft.

Using a factor of 1.4 for circulation space, closets, etc., find a total project area for the house. Using formula (1.4):

Net area	1,830 sq. ft.
Times gross area factor	× 1.4
Total project area	2,562 sq. ft.

Select a square foot price from Table One (shown on page 5) that meets your assumed material standards. Using formulas (1.3) and (1.6):

Total project area	2,562 sq. ft.
Times cost/square foot	× $70
Total construction price	$179,340
Plus lot price (from above)	+ 140,000
Subtotal	$319,340
Plus 10% soft costs	+ 31,934
Grand total project cost	$351,274

Compare the three calculations for total project cost.

Calculation One	= $360,000
Calculation Two	= $385,000
Calculation Three	= $351,274

Even though Calculation Three is the most detailed and, therefore, probably more accurate, you would be safe in selecting a midrange number of $360,000 for use in future calculations, especially since you know it is a feasible number in the area.

Proceed with the following formulas in order to establish your loan qualifying status. Using formula (1.7):

Grand total project cost	$360,000
Less 20% equity	−72,000
Total loan amount	$288,000

Assuming mortgage interests will be slightly higher next year, select a rate of 8.00 percent for thirty years from Table Three (shown on page 7) with an amortization coefficient of $7.34. Using formula (1.8):

Total loan amount	$288,000
Times table three factor	× 7.34
Subtotal	2,113,920
Divide by 1,000	÷ 1,000
Monthly amortization payment	$2,114

Next, we assume a ratio of 35 percent for taxes and insurance (escrow). Using formula (1.9):

Monthly amortization payment	$2,114
Times 1.35 (taxes and insurance factor)	× 1.35
Approximate total monthly payment	$2,854

Determine if you can qualify for this payment. Using formula (1.11):

Total monthly payment	$2,854
Divide by gross income factor	÷0.28
Monthly gross income required	$10,193

This means you would need a total gross monthly income of $10,193 or a gross yearly household income of $122,314 to qualify for this loan under most lenders' standards.

You can bring this qualifying number down by reducing the amount you borrow. This can be done in one or more of the following ways:

1. Increase your down payment or equity in the house.
2. Reduce the total project cost:
   a. Find a less expensive lot.
   b. Lower the cost per square foot of construction by reducing material standards or using cheaper subcontractors.
   c. Reduce the area of the house.
3. Some combination of the above.

Example Two

The other and perhaps more reasonable approach to determining how much you can build is to first determine how much you can afford to pay. For this example, assume your gross monthly income is $8,000. Using formula (1.10):

Gross monthly income	$8,000
Times gross income factor	×0.28
Possible monthly payment	$2,240

Proceeding in a reverse direction from Example One, find your loan amortization amount. Using formula (1.9):

Total monthly payment	$2,240
Divide by taxes and insurance factor	÷1.35
Monthly amortization payment	$1,659

Returning to Table Three (shown on page 7) and using an inverse of formula (1.8) with the factor for an 8.00 percent, thirty-year mortgage (7.34), calculate your total loan amount. Using formula (1.8):

Monthly amortization payment	$1,659
Times 1,000	×1,000
Subtotal	$1,659,000
Divide by table three factor	÷7.34
Total loan amount	$226,022

Reduce the total loan amount by 10 percent soft costs. Using formula (1.6):

Total loan amount	$226,022
Less soft costs (total loan amount ÷11)	−20,547
Amount for lot and construction	$205,475
Less lot price	−140,000
Amount available for construction	$65,475

Obviously, $65,475 will not build the house of your dreams. You will have to invest a great deal of your own equity into the project in order to build the house you want.

Next, determine how much equity you can bring to the table. Assume you still owe $70,000 on your existing house, and the neighbor just sold his similar home for $150,000.

Value of existing home	$150,000
Less 6% brokerage fee	−9,000
Less existing mortgage amount	−70,000
Total equity	$71,000

Add your equity to the amount available for construction.

Equity from existing home	$71,000
Plus loan construction amount	+65,475
Total amount for construction	$136,475

Now you know what you can afford to spend on construction. At this point, you can move in several directions:

1. If you are determined to stay in the city, you

can look at reducing your material standards and/or area. After studying Table One (shown on page 5), you might decide that $65/square foot is as low as you want to drop the construction quality. Using formula (1.2):

Total amount for construction	$136,475
Divide by cost/square foot	÷ $65
Total area	2,099 sq. ft.

Referring back to Table Two (shown on page 6), you will see that in this area range you could build a 3 bedroom, 2 bath house and probably work in a family room if you plan very efficiently and settle for smaller room dimensions.

2. You can try to save on your lot price and apply the savings to your construction cost. With your present program for construction, calculate the amount you will need to build. Using formula (1.2):

Total area	3,000 sq. ft.
Times cost/square foot	× $70
Total cost of construction	$210,000

Calculate the total amount you have to spend for the project by adding the loan amount (from above) and your own equity.

Loan amount available for lot and construction	$205,475
Plus equity	+ 71,000
Total amount available for lot and construction	$276,475

Now, subtract the projected cost of construction to find how much money is available for the lot.

Total amount available for lot and construction	$276,475
Less total cost of construction (from above)	–210,000
Amount available for lot	$66,475

This a workable deal, but you must be willing to move out to the new developments in the suburbs and look for a lot out there. The schools are good, there are lots of friends for your children, golf courses are close, and so what if you have a little commute every day.

3. You can consider a combination of 1 and 2:
   a. Reduce the size slightly.
   b. Reduce the quality slightly.
   c. Look for a less expensive lot.
   d. Throw in more personal savings.
   e. Pray for lower interest rates.
4. You can go to the boat show.

CHAPTER ONE REVIEW

How to start the process: Steps to take to get started building your home and a chart that outlines the home building process.

Construction costs: Typical new residential construction costs, ranging from $50/square foot to over $150/square foot, but averaging around $70/square foot.

Typical home sizes and areas: Typical areas of formula houses, ranging from 1,000 square feet for a 2 bedroom, 1 bath cottage up to 3,500 square feet for a 4 bedroom, 3½ bath house. Alternate methods of calculating the expected area of your house.

Land costs: Methods for determining how to price your prospective lot and formulas to calculate how much you can afford to pay.

Loans and mortgages: Formulas for calculating your monthly payment, including taxes and insurance. Loan qualification formulas used by banks.

What you can afford: Examples of how to use lending institution formulas to determine your qualification potential for the loan you need. Methods of bringing your project in line with your budget.

FINANCIAL CONSIDERATIONS

> **In this chapter, we will cover:**
>
> ✔ Selling your existing home   ✔ Types of lenders
> ✔ Contract contingencies   ✔ Money flow
> ✔ Types of loans   ✔ Payments to your contractor

Referring back to Figure 1-1 (on page 4), it is apparent that there is much to do, but many tasks can run concurrently with one another at this stage of the project.

SELLING YOUR PRESENT HOME

Certain real estate companies specialize in your area and your type of home. You can find out their names by driving around your neighborhood and checking which signs appear most often. Call them and inform them that you are considering placing your home on the market. They will send an agent to your home for an interview and to evaluate your house. Select an agent that you like personally and who seems interested in investing some energy into your sale. The agent will give you tips on various items to touch up to get the best return on your property, and he or she will inform you of a market value range for the property. Once you have an agreement, the broker will lead you through the sales process and advise you of your options. A brokerage fee, typically 6 percent, will be charged for the real estate listing and service and will come off the top of your sales proceeds at the closing.

BEGINNING YOUR SEARCH FOR YOUR NEW SITE

You should initiate this stage as quickly as possible as it may take some amount of time to find the right lot at the right price. If you find the lot before you sell your house, you can usually sign a contract for it contingent upon the sale of your property with a certain time limit. See Chapter Three—Finding Your New Home Site—for more details.

NEGOTIATING WITH YOUR LENDERS

The previous exercise in Chapter One might be called the "pro forma" of the project, which means you have created a financial model or form of the hard costs (actual construction expenses) and soft costs (consultant fees, legal fees, loan points, etc.) attributable to the project, and you have also determined how those costs will be covered (by your loan and equity) and how the loan will be amortized (by your monthly payments).

These are rough figures at this point, but they will serve you well in your next step—the visit to the bank.

Any type of construction project in the United States will require two separate loans (and sometimes three), usually from separate lenders:

1. Land loan—from the bank
2. Construction loan—from the bank
3. Mortgage loan—from a savings and loan/ mortgage company

The reason for this complexity in borrowing is because a construction project has a much higher degree of risk for the lender than does an existing building and because of the difference in length for the different loans. Different lending institutions have different risk levels they are willing to accept, and correspondingly different interest rates they are looking for.

A construction project has many moving parts and although most proceed with no real complications, anything can happen. Your contractor may get hit on the head with a falling hammer or go broke on another job and lose his credit rating with his vendors. Because of all this potential for disaster, a construction loan will be at a higher interest rate. Luckily, it is also over a shorter period of time. These loans are usually handled by the banks, who specialize in this type of short-term, high-risk, commercial investment.

A finished project without liens and lawsuits is considered a much safer investment because it is secured by an established income-producing property with a firm value in the marketplace. Therefore, a lower interest rate and a longer period of amortization is justified. Again, this more conservative type of loan package is usually handled by those institutions that specialize in these low-risk, long-term investments with smaller returns, that is, savings and loan associations or mortgage companies.

All the lending officers will be impressed by your financial pro forma and, if you have found the right institution for the range of your desired loan, will be eager to assist you in the eventual preparation of your loan package.

The loan for your lot will cover approximately 80 percent of the purchase price of the lot. You will be expected to come up with the other 20 percent from your savings or equity from the sale of your existing house. This land loan will be arranged with the understanding that you will construct a new house on it within a certain frame of time. When you begin the actual construction, your construction loan will pay off the original land loan and also pay the construction expenses. The same lender that provided your interim land loan may also provide your construction loan.

At this time, you would be requesting only a verbal statement that your numbers are in order and a nonbinding commitment that the institution would generally accept your package at the proper time. You may be able to find a better deal somewhere else by the time you need it, but it is impor-

tant that you have a financial officer check things over for any outstanding issues at the outset. The fewer surprises the better.

MONEY FLOW

Figure 2-1 maps out the flow of money through the project. Obviously you will need to put up quite a bit of money at the front end to get things rolling. Your savings will be required to fix up the existing house for sale, and once sold, your equity and some savings will be needed for the following expenditures:

1. Land down payment
2. Points and fees associated with the loans
3. Project down payment
4. Designers' fees
5. House rent during construction period

Once all the above items are funded and you have your set of house plans finished, you are ready to make application for the construction loan. You must submit your plans to the bank for a value appraisal and file the proper applications. As soon as your construction loan is approved, you should be ready to award the contract to the successful bidder and begin demolition of any existing structures.

CONTRACTOR PAYMENTS

The construction loan will list you as the owner of the project (land and improvements) and the lender as the first mortgage holder. The general contractor will make periodic "draw" requests to the bank against your loan for partial payments as the construction proceeds. The bank will assign an agent to inspect the amount of work completed and materials on site and ensure they correspond to what is shown on the contractor's request for payment. If approved, the contractor is usually paid on a retention basis; he receives 90 percent of the value of the work completed and materials used, with 10 percent held out of each payment. This 10 percent retainage insures that the contractor does not lose interest in your job before he is finished.

Half of this retained amount may be paid to the contractor upon "substantial completion" of the project, that is, when the owner and bank officially accept the project. However, some retention should be carried after the move-in date to make sure that

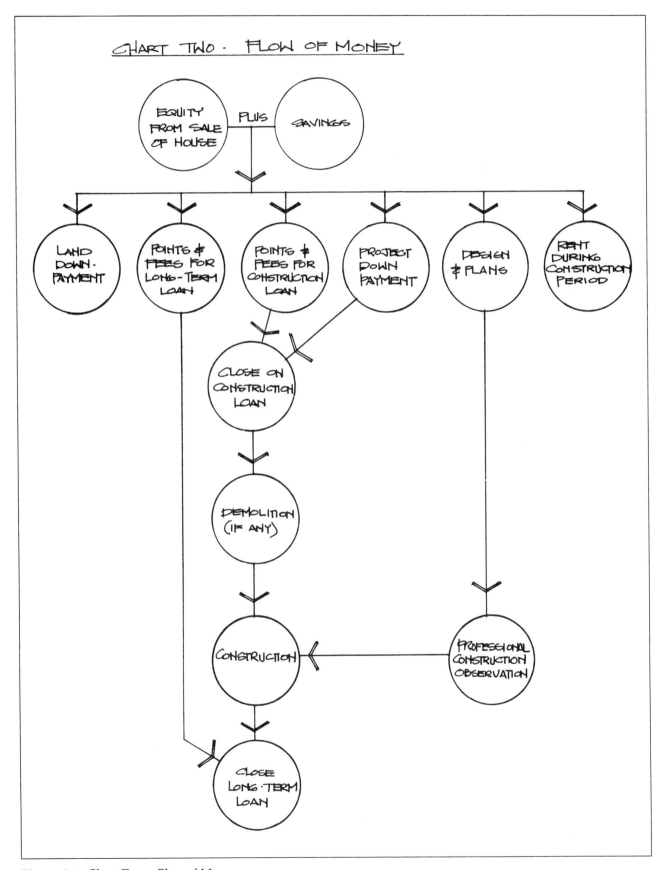

Figure 2-1: *Chart Two—Flow of Money*

the contractor finishes his final "punch list" (the list of items remaining to be fixed before his work is complete). Usually, thirty days is sufficient for an owner to live in and test the house before the final payment is made.

By this time, you should have negotiated a long-term mortgage loan for the project with another lender. When the project is finished, the money from that institution will pay off your construction loan, ending the financial wheeling and dealing on the project as far as the owner is concerned. Now all you have to do is meet the monthly payments and live happily ever after.

CHAPTER TWO REVIEW

Selling your existing home: How to select your broker and what to look for.

Contract contingencies: How to tie up the lot you want to purchase without liability until you sell your existing home.

Types of loans: A discussion of the different types of loans you may need—lot loan, construction loan, mortgage loan.

Types of lenders: A review of which institutions to approach for the different types of loans.

Money flow: Where the money will probably come from and where it will probably go.

Payments to your contractor: How the contractor can be paid in part, with money held in retention by you until the job is completed.

CHAPTER 3

FINDING YOUR NEW HOME SITE

In this chapter, we will cover:

✔ *Urban lots* ✔ *Country lots*
✔ *Suburban lots* ✔ *Site selection considerations*

Most people want to jump right into designing the house as soon as they have decided to build. This can be a fine exercise to help organize your thoughts, but keep in mind that the lot you finally purchase will almost always have a critical impact on your plan in terms of dimensions, site access, views, tree locations, slopes, etc.

Therefore, the next step in the proper sequence of things is to begin the search for the lot, negotiate the price of the lot, and write a contract to purchase the lot contingent upon the sale of your existing home.

Figure 3-1 shows the three basic types of lots, urban, suburban and country, and the main steps in site selection for each type.

URBAN LOT

The urban lot is usually smaller, but with mature trees and located within an established neighborhood. It is usually closer to the center of the city with shorter commuting distances and fewer traffic jams. This lot can usually be purchased directly from the owner, but it often has an existing structure that must be demolished or removed. This demolition can add as much as $5,000 to the price of your lot. Those lots within the better neighborhoods are more expensive, but tend to hold their value better in economic downturns. Because of the structuring of the loan package, existing structures cannot be demolished until the construction loan

is in place, which may add a few weeks to your construction time.

SUBURBAN LOT

The suburban lot is usually in a new neighborhood or development out on the edges of the city with its own shopping areas, recreational developments, schools, and so forth. These lots are larger with more frontage on the street, but less well treed and offer a longer commuting distance from the city center with the associated traffic congestion. The lots often come with deed restrictions specifying such things as minimum areas for homes, exterior finish materials and minimum construction values.

Many or all of these lots may be purchased directly from the development company. Often, the development company will have a list of approved builders from which they would like you to choose, or they will retain the right to approve the contractor you do select. Many times a home building contractor will purchase several lots for his own inventory. He will construct speculative homes on these lots (new houses that are finished before they are sold), or he will sell one to a buyer (you) with the agreement that he will build the project. In this sort of negotiated construction price arrangement, the owner has little assurance that he is obtaining the best possible price for the work. The only check will be that the contractor's price cannot exceed the bank appraisal for the value of the finished project.

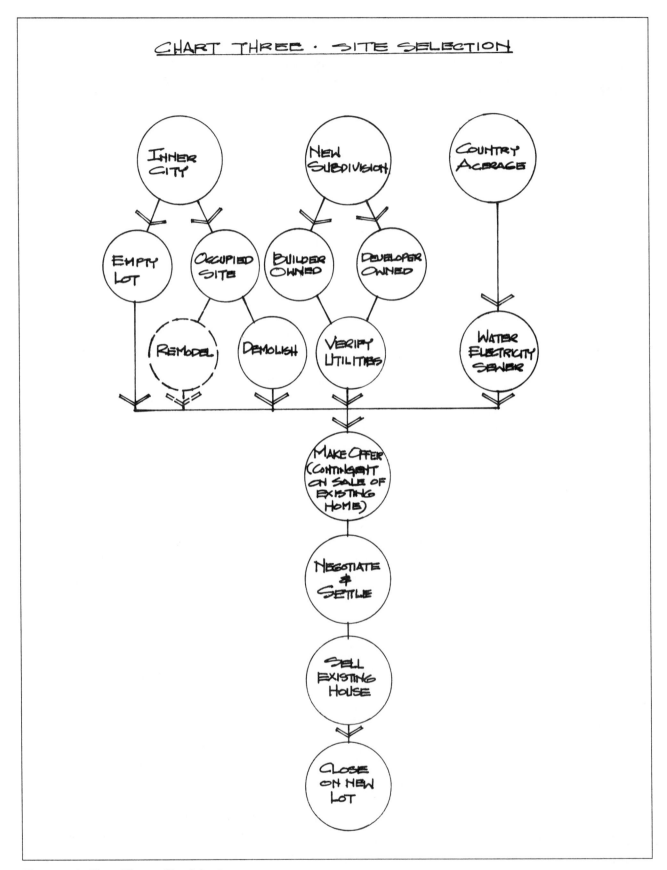

Figure 3-1: *Chart Three—Site Selection*

COUNTRY LOT

The country lot is similar to the suburban lot, but is larger, less expensive, and farther from the city center. Electricity will be delivered to your site by the local utility company as part of its service; however, you will have to provide your own water and sanitary sewage system. These utilities can be successfully accomplished with a water well (add $1,000-$2,000, depending upon depth) and a septic system for sewage disposal (add $2,500).

I recently designed a beach house for a client who had purchased a beautiful 200-acre peninsula extending out into the Gulf of Mexico and wanted to build the house out at the very tip of the land mass. There was a fine beach on both sides of the peninsula, but the land on the ridge was so thick with spiney underbrush that we could not get to the actual house site without heavy equipment.

Without a soils test, I designed the house assuming a typical hurricane zone pier foundation jetted into a sand mass. Luckily, one of the bidding contractors managed to get a small hand auger close to the site and made an exploratory boring. He found that below a five-foot layer of shell and sand was a layer of peat too deep for his equipment to find the bottom. This was alarming in itself and none of the bidders could price a foundation without a complete subsurface investigation. Ultimately, we had to put in a two-mile road (paid for out of the client's pocket) in order to get the testing equipment into the site to determine what menace lurked below the surface. We designed a foundation using thirty-five-foot treated wood piers driven twenty-five feet below the finish grade. This greatly increased the foundation costs, but it was lucky to have the information provided to us before the bids were due. Unfortunately, the contractor who had gone the extra mile was the high bidder and did all that work for nothing. Sometimes the world just isn't fair.

Just as in the design of the house, the site selection should also take resale considerations into account. Following is a checklist of important considerations in selecting the proper site.

Once you have selected a lot, all that is left to do is negotiate a final price with the owner, sell your existing home, and find another place to live during the construction period.

The time between placing your existing home on the market and when you finally sell can be put to good use. Now that the project is becoming more a reality than a dream, there is abundant incentive to begin the planning of your new home in earnest.

SITE SELECTION CHECKLIST

Sociological Considerations:
☐ School district
☐ Commuting distance to work
☐ Traffic congestion at peak hours
☐ Neighborhood amenities
☐ Neighborhood problems
☐ Recent neighborhood trends (up or down)
☐ Police response time
☐ General security
☐ Spot zoning (apartments or commercial mixed with single family)

Physical Considerations:
☐ Established trees and landscaping
☐ Drainage
☐ Size and shape
☐ Easements
☐ Excessive slopes
☐ Potential foundation problems
☐ Existing buildings
☐ Existing utilities
☐ Deed restrictions
☐ Zoning restrictions
☐ Views
☐ Solar orientation

CHAPTER THREE REVIEW

Lot types: The advantages and disadvantages of the various lot types (urban, suburban and country).

Site selection considerations: A checklist of sociological and physical qualities and characteristics to help you evaluate your site.

CHAPTER 4

PLANNING YOUR NEW HOME

In this chapter, we will cover:	
✔ Assembling design information	✔ Programming questionnaire
✔ Organizing your program	✔ Plan amenities
✔ Plan types	✔ Plan diagrams

The planning process is an evolutionary procedure of discovery and change. No one waits until the plan is exactly right in his head and then draws that vision on paper. The plan is a dialogue between the paper and the designer; it unfolds and changes as it proceeds.

Therefore, it is not so important how or where you begin to plan because sooner or later you will arrive at the plan that works best for you. The only difference in starting places is how much time it takes to get where you want to go and how much frustration you encounter on the way.

START YOUR SCRAPBOOK

The best way to begin to think about the character of your house and to convey those thoughts to another person is to browse through home magazines and collect each photograph that appeals to you and represents the type of character you want in your new home. Start a scrapbook of these photographs, organize it by subject matter or rooms, add to it, and discard ideas that lose their appeal. Collect details like shelving ideas, handrails, windows, and anything else that strikes your fancy, even if it is contradictory to other ideas in your collection.

Once the scrapbook is under way, you are ready to review some ways to start your plan.

DESIGNING YOUR HOME YOURSELF

Let's assume that at this point you would like to begin by yourself and not be influenced by the ideas of a professional or the rigidity of a finished plan from a plan book or catalog. You should start in much the same way that you would begin under the personal guidance of a design professional, that is, with the written "program." For simplicity, you can divide the program effort into two parts: needs and wants.

Space and Area Requirements (Needs)

The space and area requirements portion of the program will be a listing similar to the exercise in Chapter One (on page 9) in which you listed each room you needed in the house, the approximate dimensions of each room, and the area of each room. You then multiplied the total area by a gross area factor to account for miscellaneous circulation space, closets, stairways, and so forth.

Set up your list in three columns, as shown below.

After combining the rooms' areas to get the net

Room	Dimensions	Area (sq. ft.)
Foyer	8' × 10'	80
Living Room	14' × 20'	280
Dining Room	14' × 17'	238
Family Room	20' × 20'	400
_____	_____	_____
_____	_____	_____
_____	_____	_____

area of the house, apply formula (1.4), Total Project Area = Net Area × Gross Area Factor, where your gross area factor is between 1.2 and 1.4.

It will help you visualize how these areas and dimensions "feel" if you measure the rooms in your existing house for comparison. Another helpful visualization tool is to visit some speculative or model homes and refer to their handout describing the sizes of the various rooms as you walk through them.

Furniture layouts are critical in the dimensioning of certain rooms. For example, you should decide the maximum number of people you will wish to sit at your dining room table and make sure the room dimensions will accommodate that size table with the appropriate number of chairs. You may already own fine pieces of furniture you definitely want to incorporate into certain rooms of your new house. Make sure each individual room is large enough to comfortably fit the required furniture and allow generous circulation space (minimum three to four feet) all around it.

When compiling the above list, you should also pay some attention to the typical "formula" for a house of this size and location. Unless you are very wealthy, it might be a mistake to design too custom a home just in case you want to sell it one day and build a larger one. As mentioned before, the lender also has a concern that the house they may eventually own can be resold easily. Therefore, if all the houses around the neighborhood have a bar, you should probably include one or a place for one in your design, even if you don't drink.

The Adjacency and Character Program (Wants)

The scrapbook of photos from home magazines will be a big part of this program because this list should describe the more abstract qualities of the space. Categories for this list include, but are not limited to, preferred adjacencies (which rooms should be close or open to one another), ceiling heights in the various main spaces, openness of the general plan and plan layout. Use the following examples to think about your own plan.

Adjacencies

Rooms that should be near other rooms:
- ☐ Breakfast room open to kitchen
- ☐ Kitchen adjacent to dining room
- ☐ Kitchen adjacent to family room
- ☐ Kitchen near garage
- ☐ Dining room near living room
- ☐ Living and dining rooms near entry foyer
- ☐ Kids' rooms near each other
- ☐ Kids' rooms share bath

Rooms that should not be near other rooms:
- ☐ Master suite distant from kids' rooms
- ☐ Master suite away from street
- ☐ Music room distant from TV room

Plan Type

- ☐ **Open plan** — Major rooms all or partially open to each other.
- ☐ **Closed plan** — Each major space clearly defined as a separate room with walls and doors.
- ☐ **Combination plan** — Kitchen, breakfast room, family room open to one another; other rooms formally distinct and closed.

Ceiling Heights

Assuming an eight-, nine-, or ten-foot ceiling height as typical for most of your house, think about which rooms, if any, should have different ceiling heights or sloped ceilings. Most newer homes are designed with ten-foot ceilings in living areas and nine-foot ceilings in bedrooms.

Plan Layout

For your particular lot, determine if there is a special view you want to see from the bedroom window, a large tree to design around, eastern (sunrise) exposure for bedrooms, etc.

Adjectives

For each major room or space, see if you can make a list of adjectives that describe how you want that room to feel, for example, cozy, warm, dark, sunny, spacious or bright. Don't worry for now if they seem to contradict one another.

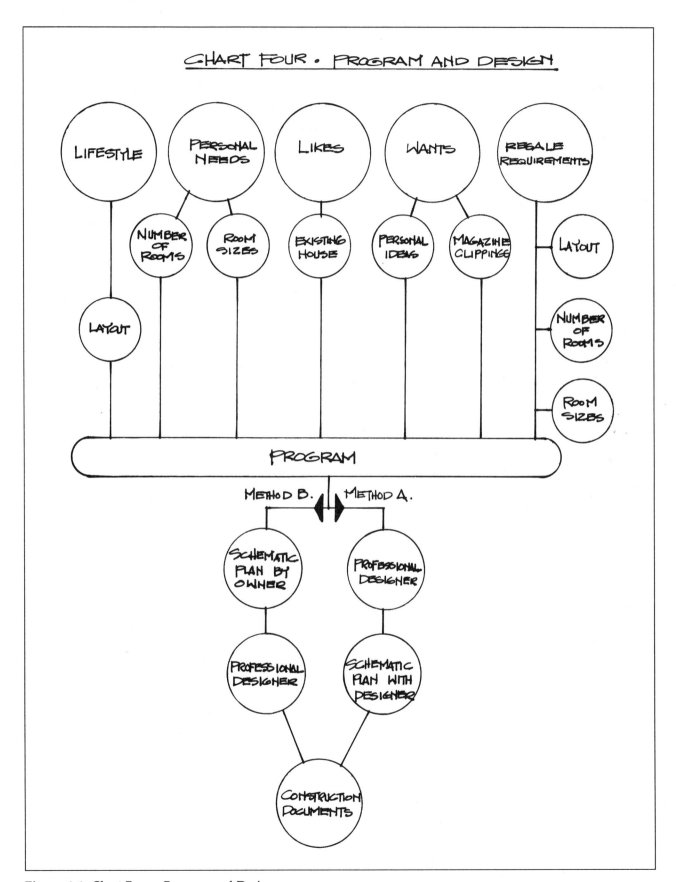

Figure 4-1: *Chart Four—Program and Design*

Figure 4-1 (on page 23) shows a chart for use in developing your program and design.

THE PROGRAMMING QUESTIONNAIRE

To help you organize your ideas, take some time to fill out the following questionnaire:

Part I: Your Current Home

Describe what you like most about your current home. _____
_____

Describe what you like least about it. _____
_____

Are there enough rooms? _____
Are the rooms large enough? _____
Which rooms are too small? _____
_____

Is your current home too dark? _____
Does the master bedroom have enough privacy?
_____

Does your current home have any recurrent maintenance problems? _____
_____

How well does the kitchen work? How could it be improved? _____
_____
_____
_____

Is there enough storage space? _____
Is the main dining area defined as a room or as an area off the living room? Does this arrangement work well for you? _____
Do you find yourself entertaining in the kitchen?
_____

Where do you and your kids watch TV? _____
_____

Part II: Your Lifestyle

1. Which sounds more appealing?
   A) Quiet, intimate retreat
   B) Large, open spaces
2. How does your family dine most often?
   A) Formally, in the dining room
   B) Informally, in the kitchen, breakfast room or family room
3. How do you entertain?
   A) Formally, in the living room and dining room
   B) Informally, in the kitchen and/or family room
   C) In the backyard
4. What do you most often do at home for personal entertainment?
   A) Watch TV
   B) Listen to music
   C) Hobbies
   D) Read
   E) Other
5. Where do you watch TV?
   A) With the kids in the family or living room
   B) In your bedroom
6. How often do you entertain? _____
7. How much privacy do you need? _____
8. How much light do you like?
   A) Shades usually open
   B) Curtains usually drawn
9. Where do you work?
   A) Always at the office
   B) Sometimes at home
   C) Always at home

Part III: Your New House Plan

1. What special rooms would you like?
   A) Woodworking shop
   B) Sewing room
   C) Butler pantry
   D) Office
   E) Library
   F) Bar
   G) Music room
   H) Studio
   I) Auto workshop
2. What amenities would you like?
   A) Master bath:
      1) Whirlpool tub
      2) Separate shower
      3) Steam or sauna room (can be combined with shower)
      4) Separate water closet room
      5) Access to master closet
   B) Family room:
      1) Built-in entertainment/storage unit
      2) Bookshelves
      3) Fireplace

C) Kitchen:
    1) Wall ovens
    2) Freezer
    3) Desk
    4) Walk-in pantry
    5) Trash compactor
    6) Center island
D) Living room:
    1) Space for piano
    2) Fireplace
    3) Bookshelves
    4) Built-in storage

Part IV: What General Character Appeals to You?

1. Open and light:
    A) Open plan
    B) High ceilings
    C) Large windows
    D) Ample lighting fixtures
    E) Light color palette
    F) Wood or tile floors
2. Cozy and shady:
    A) Defined rooms, closed plan
    B) Lower ceilings
    C) Smaller windows
    D) Switched outlets for lamps
    E) Deeper colors
    F) Plush carpets

If your answers to the first part of the questionnaire show that you are basically satisfied with your current house, then you only need to make a list of the items that could be made better such as larger rooms, more bedrooms or more windows, and the design of your new home will be a relatively simple task and easy for you to visualize. However, it is very important to remember that you are building a new house so you can have a design exactly suited for your lifestyle. The first reaction to any design problem is usually to refer to the way it happens in your present house and reproduce that situation. You should actively try not to use details of your existing home as a model for your new one unless you are very satisfied with them. Almost any condition can be improved upon with a little thought.

If your answers to the questions about your current home indicate a generally negative feeling, some of the answers should give you a clue to how it could be improved.

Go through your scrapbook of home pictures from magazines and try to determine what you like about the spaces in the photos and how they are different from the spaces in your current home. Compare your current house and another house you have visited that you found attractive. Make two columns with headings labeled "My Current Home" and "John Smith's House" (the one you liked). Note the corresponding characteristics of each home for the important spaces in the house. Use categories for comparison such as:

☐ Ceiling heights and slopes
☐ Sizes of rooms
☐ Shapes of rooms
☐ Openness to other rooms or spaces
☐ Types of windows
☐ Ratio of glass area to wall area
☐ Floor materials
☐ Wall materials
☐ Ceiling materials
☐ Floor colors
☐ Wall colors
☐ Ceiling colors
☐ Lighting (direct or indirect)
☐ Quantity of natural light
☐ Quantity of electric light
☐ Amount and type of trim
☐ Direct solar exposure
☐ Views outside

Try the same exercise with a room from your scrapbook that you particularly like. As you study the characteristics of each space and try to put them into words, you will begin to see the features that made you feel differently. You will become more aware of what you want in your new house, and you will be better able to make it happen.

In the questions concerning your lifestyle, if you answered (A) most often in the lifestyle portion, you would probably be happiest with a closed plan, in which each room has four walls and a door. You may be a more private and introspective person and prefer quietness and solitude. If you answered (B) most often in this section, you would probably prefer a more open plan, in which some areas open onto others. In this case, you may be more gregarious and social. The open plan also has the advantage of making the whole house seem larger and more spacious. Compare your results from the lifestyle section to your results from the other sections of the questionnaire.

THE BALLOON DIAGRAM

In order to help you organize your ideas and enable you to begin thinking visually, you can sketch out your adjacency program for each level of the house. You may start by drawing a circle to represent each room in the approximate location you think is best. Then connect the rooms that should be adjacent to one another with a line. You may have to move and shift the circles around a little to make it work out, but when you are finished you will have a diagram that is a close representation to a plan for your house. Figures 4-2 and 4-3 show you sample adjacency programs for a two story house.

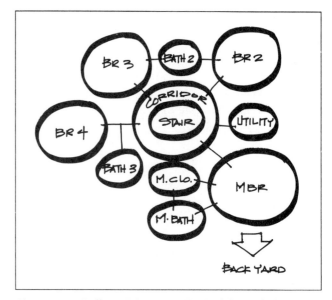

Figure 4-3: *Balloon Diagram — Typical Second Floor*

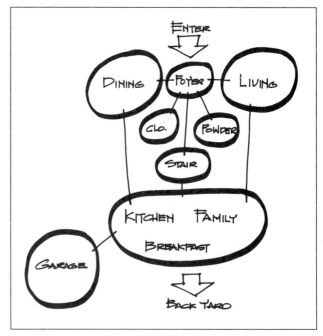

Figure 4-4: *Balloon Diagram — First Floor Alternate*

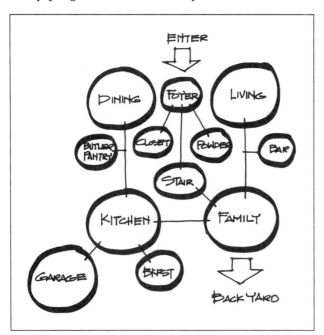

Figure 4-2: *Balloon Diagram — Typical First Floor*

Of course, since it is your house, you can utilize totally different notions in different areas of the house. For example, you may want a very formal living and dining area for business entertaining, but a very informal and open kitchen, breakfast and

family room area for the family quarters. In this case, your balloon diagram would look something like Figure 4-4 (above).

These diagrams are very quick and simple methods to help you think and organize your thoughts. At this point, you could take your ideas and scrapbook to a design professional, and you will have streamlined the programming process a great deal for the designer. You will be able to be more firm in your decisions about how the spaces should be arranged and more knowledgeable about how you want the major spaces to feel. You may even have a very rough sketch for a plan after a few passes at a balloon diagram. If your designer is working on an hourly basis, this exercise will definitely provide you with a great savings in design dollars and a feeling that you know what you are doing.

The advantage of seeing a design professional at this stage is that the plan is still fluid, and the designer will have more flexibility to coordinate the massing and exterior elevations with a developing plan. The early dialogue between plan and three-dimensional massing before too many decisions are too firmly set will produce a superior project in the end.

Bear in mind that a well-designed building is not the result of a great plan that someone has merely extended into the third dimension. It is the successful combination of plan, massing and elevation, which must be cooked together to produce the right result.

If you decide to wait until you have worked the plan out exactly like you want it before you take it to a professional, it may actually take the designer more time to make your plan work well in mass and elevation than if he had been able to work it out himself from the beginning. And if you have labored long hours to make a part of your plan work, you may be hesitant to toss it out and head in another direction if that is necessary.

For a professional to design an efficient plan is a relatively simple task and does not consume much time. Therefore, grinding out the finished plan yourself will ultimately save no time and little, if any, money.

But, if you decide to continue to develop your ideas by yourself, it can be a very valuable learning process and greatly rewarding, if not sometimes frustrating for the beginner.

CHAPTER FOUR REVIEW

Assembling design information: Suggestions on collecting design ideas for a "scrapbook" to help you visualize what you want in your home.

Organizing your program: Methods to use when writing and constructing your program, including visualization techniques and priority development.

Plan types: Basic plan organizational techniques to fit basic personality types.

Programming questionnaire: Questions to stimulate your thought process and to help you focus on the important issues of your program and the organization of your new house.

Plan amenities: A checklist of potential extras you may not want to forget when planning your new home.

Plan diagrams: A simple, quick, step-by-step system by which you can transform your program ideas into a graphic organization that you can then evolve into an actual rough plan.

CHAPTER 5

HOUSE PLAN SOURCES

In this chapter, we will cover:

✔ Plan books
✔ Home kit brochures
✔ Do-it-yourself plans (additive and subtractive methods)

✔ The use of professional assistance — how much you need

In order to continue by yourself, there are four basic directions to choose from, all leading to the same place. You can use plan books, home kit brochures, do-it-yourself plans, and/or hire professional assistance.

PLAN BOOKS

Plan books may be the most straightforward path to get you where you want to go. Any popular bookstore in your area will have a section on houses, home improvement, architecture, etc., wherein you will find a variety of house plan books. Each page will contain a perspective drawing of the finished house (or an actual photograph) and the corresponding floor plans to the house. These books vary mainly in the type of house covered. You will find books specializing in the following house types:

☐ Log homes
☐ Cottages
☐ Two story neo-classical homes
☐ Vacation homes
☐ Ranch style suburban homes
☐ Sprawling mansions

Take a few minutes to study each book in the store, and make sure it contains the plans for the type of house you want to build. Also, make sure at least some of the plans inside are compact enough to fit within the setback lines on your lot. Many of these homes are designed for very large suburban lots and will not work on a smaller urban lot without drastic change.

From the table of contents, select the chapters that correspond to your desired house type by number of bedrooms, baths, etc. As you study the plans, you will begin to see similarities between them and your balloon diagram. You will also notice that many plans in the book are very similar to one another.

If you are lucky enough to find the exact plan that suits your wants and needs and you like the character of the exterior drawing or picture of the house, you have come to the right place and you will save some money on your construction plans.

You can send off for a complete builder set of plans for that house from the publisher. The prices vary according to the size of the house and what kind of prints you order, but a typical price will be $600 for a set of reproducible sepia plans from which you can make any amount of blue-line copies for pricing and construction.

These plans should be complete enough for building permit approval. If not, the publisher usually offers a drafting service at an hourly rate, or your contractor can recommend or supply a drafting service.

The biggest problem you may encounter with this venture is that it will be very difficult to find the "exact" plans for your needs, wants and site. After enough study of any plan in the book, you will realize that many improvements could be made to make it work better for you and your lot. The bathroom would work better over there, the living room location does not take advantage of the view, the garage is on the wrong side of the house, or the master bedroom should have a larger closet.

The company that sold you the book will also offer customizing services to make minor changes to the plan for a fee, or you can contact a local design professional to make the changes (see Chapter Six).

Keep in mind that any change to the plan will almost always change the elevations, sections, foundation plan, roof framing plan, and so forth, all the way through the drawings. The plan book may have been a good place to start, but when you finish you may have a patched up set of drawings that is no longer space efficient, does not function well, looks compromised from the exterior and costs too much. Be careful.

HOME KIT BROCHURES

Prefabricated or kit homes are another good way to save on plans and possibly construction costs, since many of these homes are fabricated in panels in a factory and assembled on site by local contractors experienced with the prefab company's systems.

One example of this type of service is Jim Walter Homes, with offices all over the southern and eastern United States. This company has model homes at its office locations or will send you a catalog of plans and photos upon request.

Jim Walter specializes in a very straightforward, no-frills house for the budget-minded. The salespeople are draftsmen capable of customizing the plan you buy and loan officers capable of financing your construction through the company. If there is no office in your location, you can order a catalog from:

Jim Walter Homes
P.O. Box 31601
Tampa, Florida 33631-3601

The house parts are assembled by a local contractor familiar with the Jim Walter system. Construction price depends on percentage of comple-

tion; the maximum completion rate available is 90 percent (Jim Walter's figure). The owner is responsible for finishing the project, such as completing electrical and plumbing hookups, taping and floating interior walls, doing trim work and painting. This all amounts to a large order.

The unfinished prices may seem inexpensive, but remember the old adage: "It takes 50 percent of the time to do 90 percent of the work, and the other 50 percent of the time to do the last 10 percent of the work." This package might be very appealing to the handyman building a small home in the country; he can do a lot of the work himself and will settle for less than perfect in the finished job.

For those more interested in grand or upscale finished homes, a company such as Acorn Structures, Inc. should be able to fit your needs, within their specific construction system. Acorn Structures (and other companies like it) offers a complete home design and construction package organized around a prefabricated wall panel system that can be erected by man power only. The package includes "all structural components, siding and exterior trim, windows and doors, roofing materials, cabinets and interior trim, nails, hardware, and a variety of specialized items." The panels are fabricated in Acorn's factories with windows and doors in place. Once the house is "dried in" or weatherproof, the heating, plumbing, electrical, insulation and finish trades complete the job in the same manner as a built-from-scratch custom home.

Acorn Structures' representatives will send you a catalog of plans and photos, visit your site, and work with you as would a design professional to customize your plan or to develop your own custom house plan. For this service, Acorn requests a "design deposit" of $1,000-$4,000, depending upon the amount of work involved, and will deduct this design cost from the price of the house.

The actual construction will be done by a local contractor. Acorn will provide support services for your local builder to insure that the system is properly assembled.

While these projects are high in quality and often very handsome architecturally, you will probably never sit down across the table from your designer. In the end, although it may not cost you more, you may not save any real money over the standard design-build process, and you have given up an amount of control over the project.

Acorn information can be requested by writing to:

Acorn Structures, Inc.
P.O. Box 1445
Concord, Massachusetts 01742

DO-IT-YOURSELF PLANS: ADDITIVE METHOD

If you want to continue to develop your conceptual balloon diagram without help, you may want to use a method I call the "additive method." For this method you will use copies of the gridded paper in the back of this chapter (page 47) as a base for your plan. (Use the grid at 100%.) The grid squares are ¼″ × ¼″ or four equal spaces to an inch. This corresponds to the architect's scale of ¼″ = 1′. At this scale, each ¼″ box represents a 1′ box on the plan: a 2″ × 2″ box would represent an 8′ × 8′ room.

To continue this exercise, you will need some supplies. Make a trip to you local art supply store and purchase a roll of translucent paper (referred to as tracing paper, trash paper or butter paper), an architect's scale and a good eraser. These items can be purchased for less than $10.

Tear off a sheet of the translucent paper and lay it over the gridded page. Using the grid as your scale dimension guide, draw each room in your program list according to the dimensions from the list. Label each room's drawing. Now, cut out the rooms you drew and lay them on the table. Figure 5-1 (page 35) shows how your "parts" should look.

Remember, the total area of your rooms (net area) will be about 75 percent of the gross total area of the house because we still must add in space for storage and miscellaneous circulation.

Using your site survey for a model, draw a site plan of your lot similar to Figure 5-2 (page 36), at the same scale of your cutouts. Make sure you include the following information on your site plan.

Front building line: Any urban or suburban lot will have a front building line, beyond which you cannot build. This will mark the front boundary of your construction.

Side yard setback lines: As with your front building line, urban or suburban lots will have minimum setbacks from the side property lines, usually three to five feet.

Rear yard setback line: Your rear yard setback line marks the rear boundary of your construction. Setback lines are determined by the city planning requirements and your property deed restrictions.

Natural slopes: If your lot has any steep slopes or gullies, mark them on your site plan and either avoid them or use them to your advantage.

North arrow: All plans, including your site plan, should have the north arrow clearly marked for orientation to the other plans, room finish schedule notations, and sun position reference.

Location of major trees: The major trees on your lot will be one of your greatest assets if used correctly in the planning of your house. Mark them on your plan and ask your nurseryman how close you can safely build without harm to the root system.

Direction of views: Use arrows to mark the direction of any good views from your site, and plan your house to take advantage of them.

Garage access: Mark how you will enter your site with your driveway. This will impact your planning in a major way. Many property deed restrictions include controls for the location and orientation of garages.

Now, place your cutouts on your site plan and move them around until they seem to be in the correct locations with regard to your balloon diagram and any specific features of the site itself, as shown in Figures 5-3 and 5-4 (pages 37-38). Again, you are only concerned with the major spaces at this point. The auxiliary areas such as corridors and closets will be worked into the in-between spaces later. Be sure all rooms needing outside windows have an exterior wall.

If you are designing a two or three story house, it is important that the stairs, fireplace chimney, etc., line up for vertical connection, and that some walls line up vertically for structural support to the roof.

When you are satisfied that you have all the rooms in the proper position, it may be necessary to shift or reshape them slightly in order to form a more cohesive plan, as shown in Figures 5-5 and 5-6 (pages 39-40). Lay another piece of your tracing paper over your cutouts and sketch the changes, stretching here and compacting there, adding access corridors and storage space as you search for order. If you need a larger piece of paper, it can be purchased at any art supply store.

The next overlay will be further refinements and adjustments for access, storage and order. This means lining up walls that are already close to being lined up, subdividing storage areas between the various rooms, and checking for access to secondary spaces. The diagrams shown in Figures 5-7 and 5-8 (pages 41-42) begin to resemble a plan.

Furniture Layouts

After a series of overlay refinements, you will arrive at a plan that begins to satisfy your basic requirements in terms of room sizes, storage areas, zoning and efficiency. Now, you should test it for your particular lifestyle by laying out in the proper scale the openings, furniture and appliances in each room. This becomes very important in the case of focal elements such as antique furniture pieces, fireplaces, televisions or major art pieces. Place your tracing paper with the room drawn on it over the ¼" scale typical furniture and appliance templates in Figure 5-9 (page 43), and arrange the interior the way you want it. (Note: Figure 5-9 was reduced from its original size to fit in this book. All images in Figure 5-9 should be enlarged at 130% to provide accurate sizes for this exercise.)

Pay close attention to how the furnishings relate to the doors and windows in the room. Make certain you leave three to four feet between tables and walls for chair pulls and circulation space. See Figure 5-10 (page 44) for an example layout in the family room.

When the furniture layout works, you can add details such as electrical outlets, switches, telephone jacks, cable TV jacks and stereo speaker jacks.

DO-IT-YOURSELF PLANS: SUBTRACTIVE METHOD

There is another design method worth mentioning that is more useful if you already know what shape the exterior of the house should take. This method can be called the "subtractive method." You will use the same translucent paper placed over the grid paper as we did before. The difference is that this time you will start with the preconceived exterior shape and area of your choice, and subdivide the interior into the various rooms you need.

Your exterior shape can be defined by your lot setback lines or simply a rectangle of the proper area you wish to construct. Figure 5-11 (page 45) shows how this might work for a rectangular shape.

Since the exterior wall is a major contributor to the overall cost of the project, this method is a good one for controlling the exterior shape of the design and arriving at a simple and inexpensive plan.

On the other hand, the inherent rigidity of this system may hinder creative ideas and prove very frustrating to a beginning designer.

HOW MUCH PROFESSIONAL ASSISTANCE YOU NEED

Whichever method you use to arrive at your schematic plan, it is almost certain that sooner or later you will have to meet with an experienced design professional in order to convert your conceptual ideas into a set of legal construction documents and specifications and to finalize your building permit.

Exactly how much professional assistance you might require will depend on the following:
1. Project budget
2. Project size
3. Project complexity
4. Desired quality levels
5. Your own confidence
6. Your openness to new ideas
7. Your experience level in construction
8. Your available time

Project Budget

If your budget is very tight, it may dictate an extremely simple, bare-bones structure. In this situation, your builder may be the best source for design information since he will determine the price of the project, and the project design will be subservient to the price. He will usually be associated with a draftsman or residential designer who can produce the required documents for you at a good cost.

Alternately, if you have a budget that will allow for fine finish materials and detailing, it would be well worth your while to have a good designer orchestrate the project. It can be a waste of your money to afford fine materials if they are not used with assurance and skill.

If your present budget is very limited, you may want to design your new house as the first phase of your dream home with future additions to be added when you can afford them. If you decide to do this, it is very important that you design all the phases in the beginning so the ultimate plan works well. Once the total plan is satisfactory, go back and delete areas to be added back later, such as a bedroom wing or the finished build-out of an attic space. Remember to size the original spaces you build large enough to be in scale with the completed plan. Otherwise you may end up with a small house and a large addition; your final plan will be compromised by a failure to look far enough ahead.

Project Size

Large projects become more complex by their size alone, in terms of mechanical, electrical, structural systems and their coordination. Mistakes can be very costly. Also, the larger the project, the smaller the professional fee becomes relative to the total job cost.

Project Complexity

Regardless of the size of the project, a complicated design should have the input of an experienced design professional. Complicated projects should be studied in three-dimensional models and will require many more detail drawings to fully study and explain the construction to the contractor and building official.

Desired Quality Levels

Higher levels of quality demand and deserve the attention of a qualified design professional. The plan itself, the proper coordination of plan to elevations and massing, and the skillful orchestration of project details require a level of awareness not plainly evident to the typical home owner and, indeed, not totally necessary for the large majority of

houses built. Perhaps a good analogy can be found in wristwatch design: A Swatch can keep exact time, but a Cartier is a thing of beauty. If you cannot afford more than minimum standards or cannot tell the difference, you probably do not need more than a minimum level of professional assistance.

Your Own Confidence

If you really feel that you know exactly what you need and want in a house and just want someone to "draw it up" for you, you will probably need only minimal professional assistance.

Your Openness to New Ideas

Even if you know exactly what you want and need, if you are flexible enough to consider modifications or variations of your concept, assistance from a skilled professional can invariably make your project a better and more efficient house. Also, regardless of the end result, you will have the satisfaction of knowing that you have explored more than one direction in arriving at your final decision.

Your Experience Level in Construction

If you are a construction or design professional, you may not need any assistance from another professional in designing your own home or drafting your permit documents. However, if you do not feel comfortable drafting your own permit documents, you will obviously want some assistance. It is not unusual even for a management-type architect to hire a design architect to assist with the design of his house because he is aware of his own limitations and aware of how beneficial skilled assistance can be.

Your Available Time

Designing your own home can absorb as much time as you can put into it, especially if you are not trained in design and in construction details and materials. It can be exciting for a while, but has every possibility of turning into a very frustrating experience. The process is loaded with countless indeterminate variables that must be considered and evaluated. Once the meter starts ticking on lot payments, interest, rental house payments, etc., your time becomes very expensive. Time saved during this period by hiring a professional can go a long way toward paying his fee.

CHAPTER FIVE REVIEW

Plan books: A discussion of house plan books available in your local bookstore, what to look for and what to expect.

Home kit brochures: Strengths and shortcomings of prefabricated home designs, the modern version of houses by mail.

Do-it-yourself plans: Step-by-step methods you can use to design your own house plans.

Additive method: An overview of a method of design in which the individual rooms of the house are drawn up, and then arranged and modified as needed to form a cohesive plan.

Subtractive method: An overview of this "reverse" method of design, in which the house's exterior shape is known first and then the interior areas are designated.

How much professional assistance you need: A discussion of your goals in your home design and what kind of professional assistance you will require to achieve them.

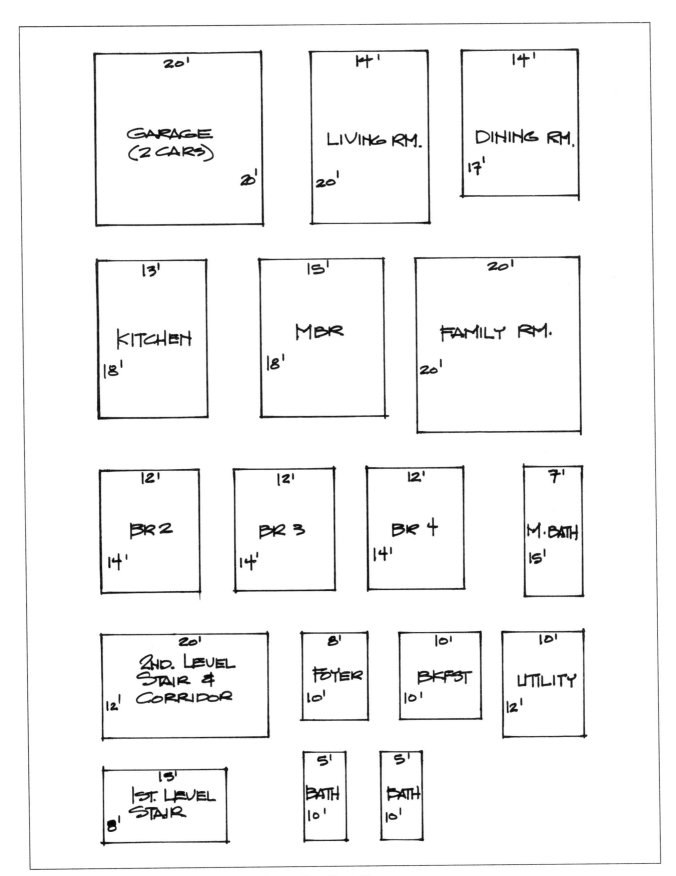

Figure 5-1: *Parts Kit for a Typical Four Bedroom, Two Story House*

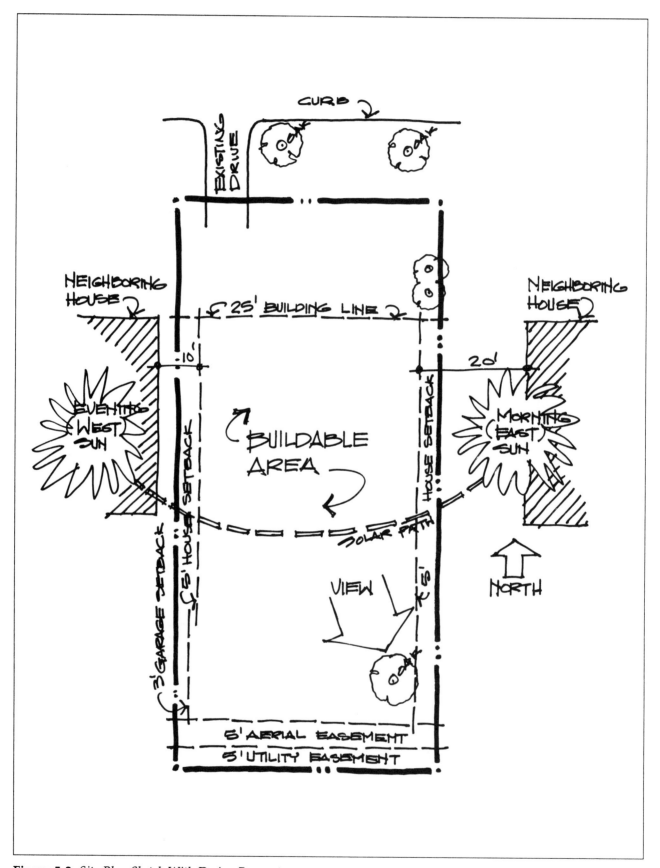

Figure 5-2: *Site Plan Sketch With Design Parameters*

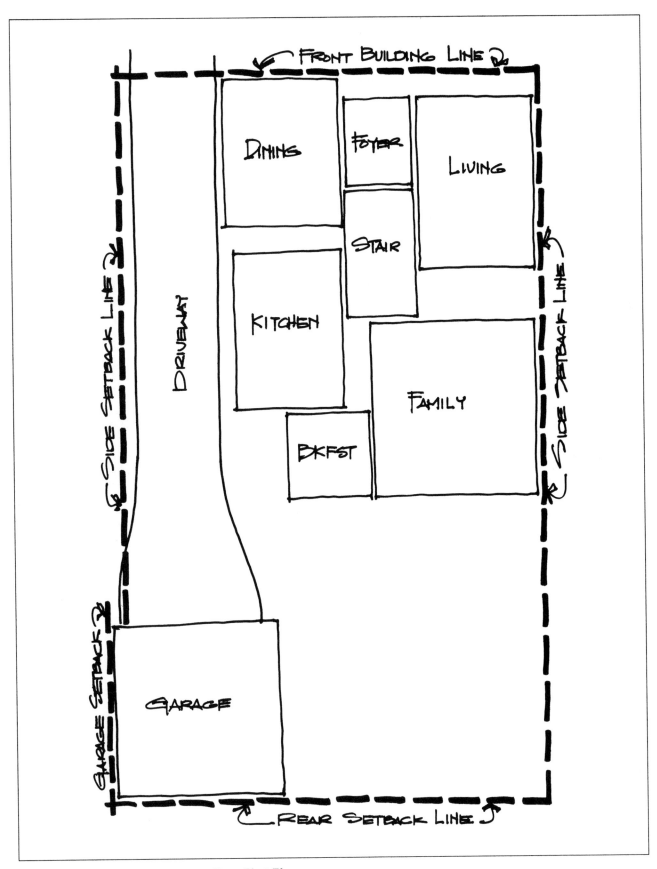

Figure 5-3: *Initial Parts Layout on Site—First Floor*

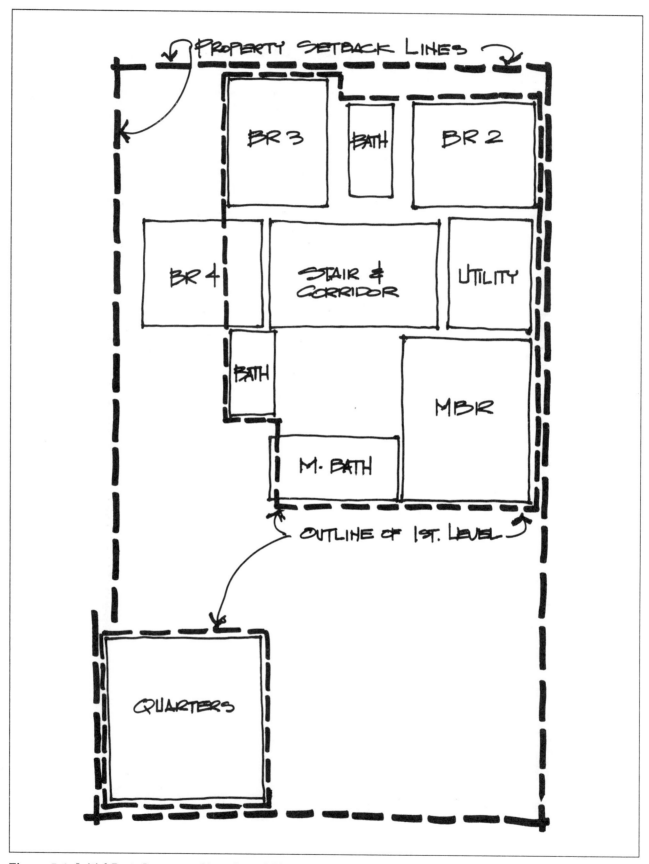

Figure 5-4: *Initial Parts Layout on Site — Second Floor*

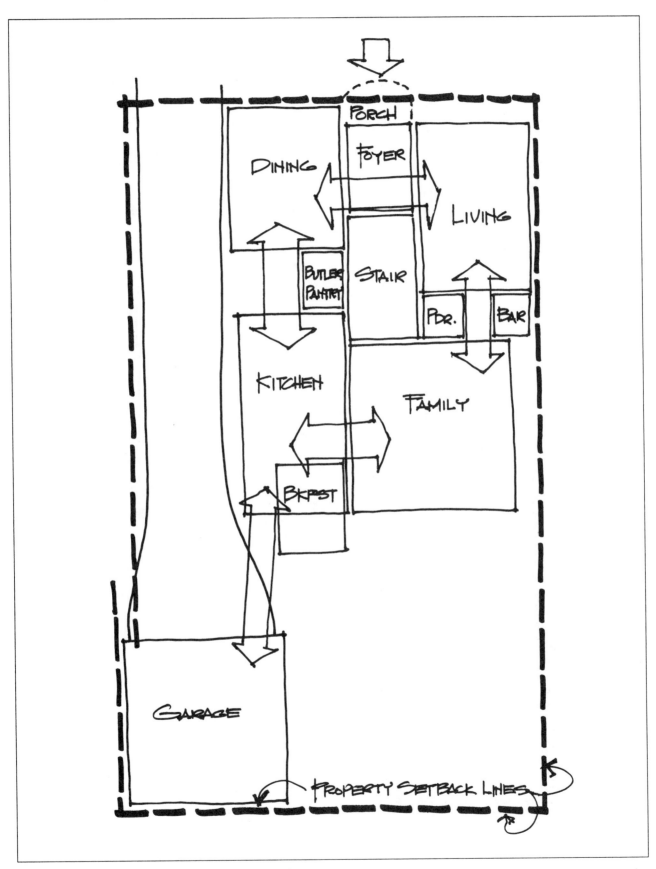

Figure 5-5: *Refinement of Parts Diagram — First Floor*

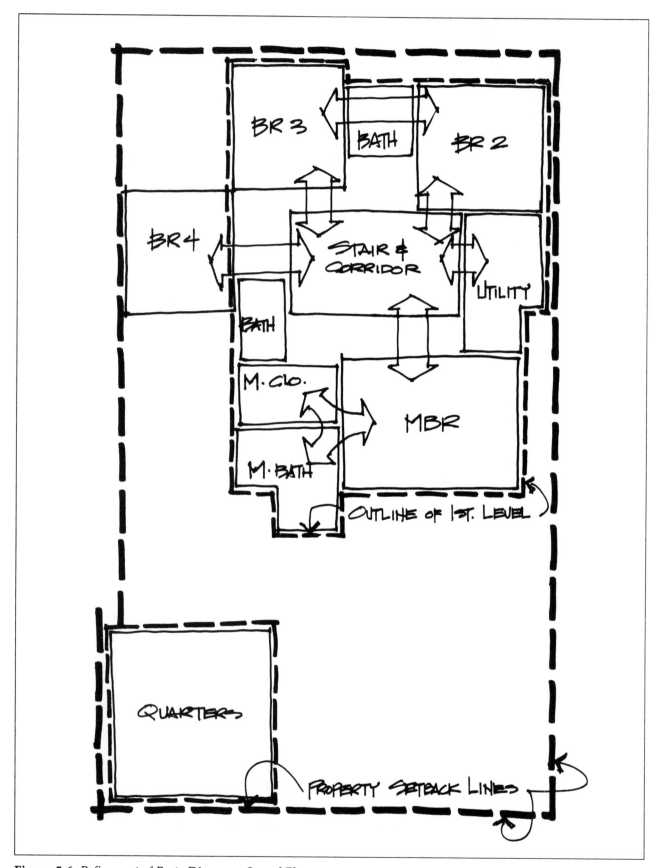

Figure 5-6: *Refinement of Parts Diagram — Second Floor*

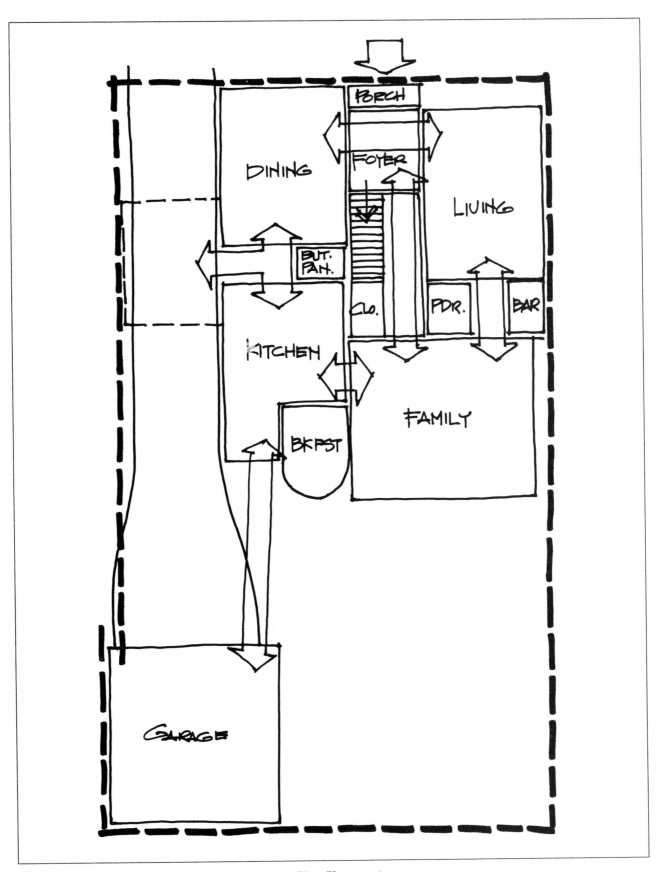

Figure 5-7: *Further Refinement of Parts Diagram — First Floor*

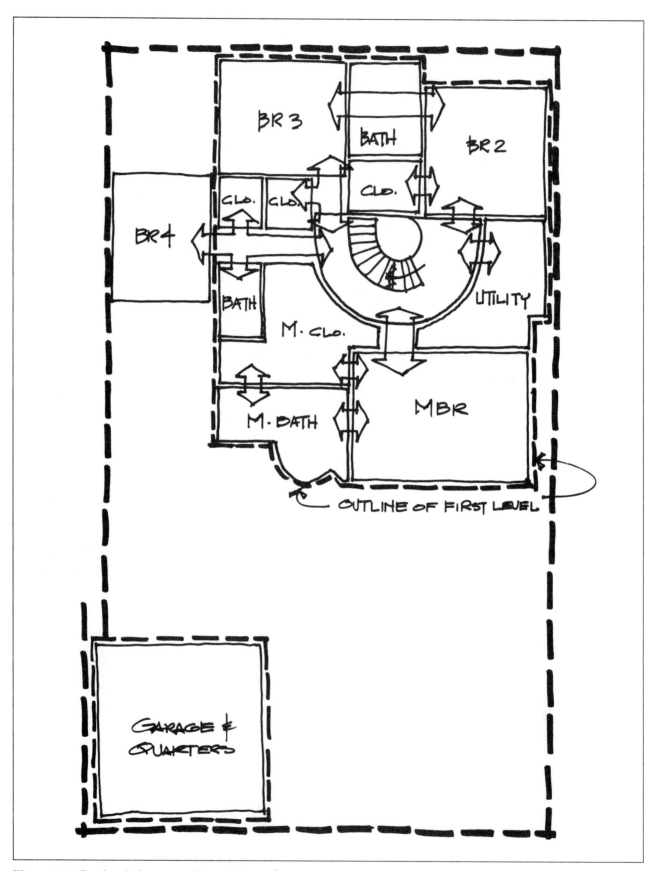

Figure 5-8: *Further Refinement of Parts Diagram—Second Floor*

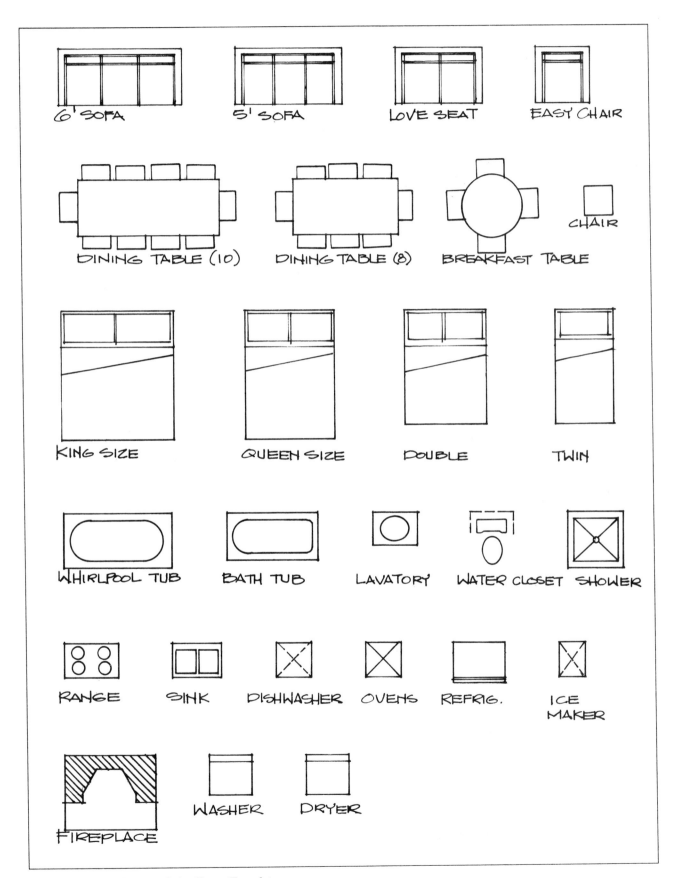

Figure 5-9: *Furniture and Appliance Templates*

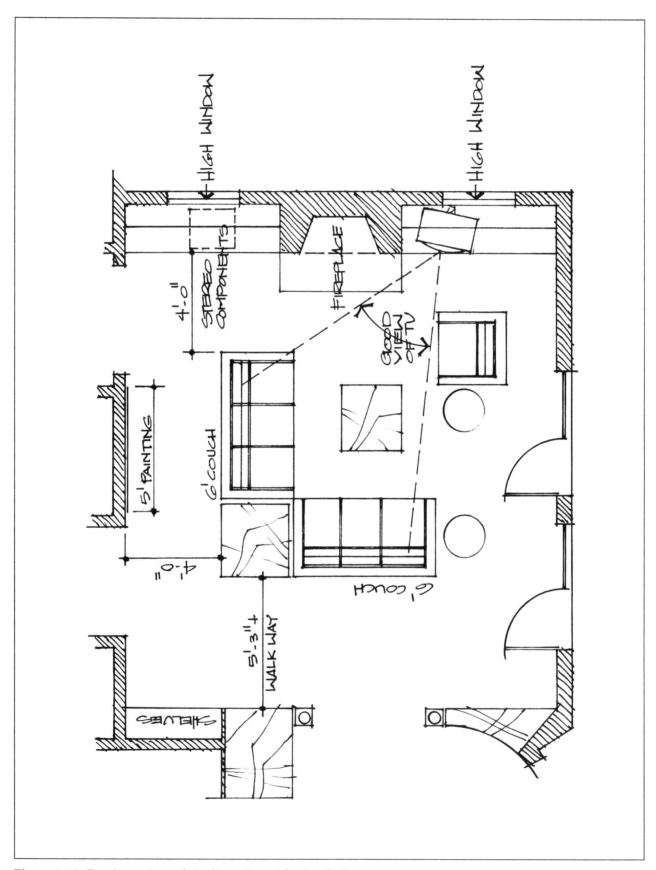

Figure 5-10: *Furniture, Art and Appliance Layout for Family Room*

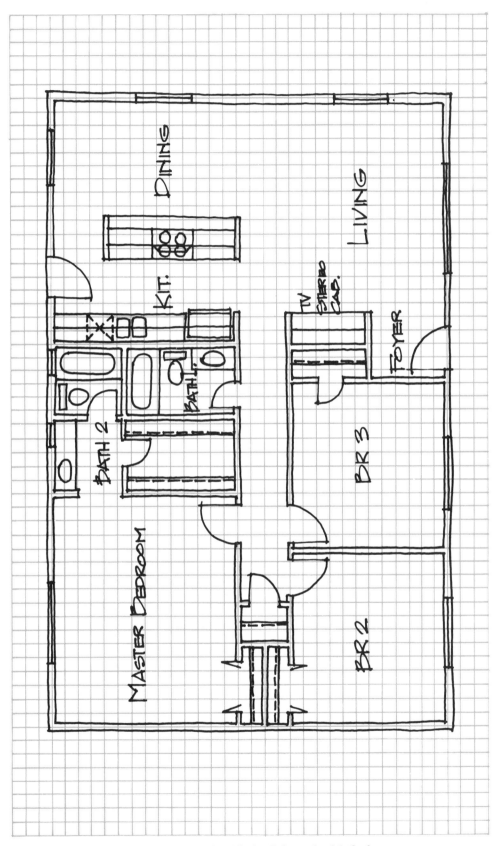

Figure 5-11: *A Simple Plan Designed With the Subtractive Method*

CHAPTER 6
PROFESSIONAL ASSISTANCE AND FEES

In this chapter, we will cover:	
✔ Types of professional designers	✔ Fee ranges
✔ Services to expect from each type	✔ Advantages and disadvantages of each type

There are many different design professionals who can help you organize your ideas into a cohesive design and into a final set of drawings for pricing, permit and construction. These professionals, in descending fee scale, are discussed as follows:

Architect
Residential Designer
Moonlight Architect
Home Builder Designer Service
Draftsman
Architectural Student

The fees charged by these professionals will be somewhat negotiable depending on how much work they have at the time and how much service you wish to purchase. Some of the variables that are important to consider when comparing fees are:

- Type of service provided
- Amount of service provided
- Educational level
- Experience level
- Reputation
- Personality
- Size of office
- References

ARCHITECT

An architect is a person who has been legally certified to use that title by the state government. Although many designers refer to themselves as architects to simplify communications, they may not be licensed as such by the state and are using the title loosely and illegally.

To become licensed as an architect, a person must complete eight years of certified training and a residency program, including college and apprenticeship, pass a grueling three-day national exam, and maintain basic ethical standards in the performance of their duties.

By far, the most important factor in the design of your home will be the communication and working relationship between you and your designer. Much of the architect's training and experience revolves around communication, and the level of service rendered by the architect includes the time for in-depth study of your project and intense sessions with you—the client.

The understanding and insight you have gained by reading this book and working through the examples should greatly enhance your communications with your architect. The designs you have produced may even be directly transformed into a final plan. Your experience will also have given you more confidence that the direction you have chosen is the correct choice, eliminating the need to explore new directions at the last minute. All this will contribute to a very efficient design phase with little or no backtracking and will save hours and hours of your designer's time and an equal amount of money.

Architect's Service

Your architect will assist you in the organization and development of your program to record your needs, wants, likes, dislikes, etc. into a comprehensive package. The previous program exercises in this book and your scrapbook will help immensely in this endeavor and will shorten the time spent and save you money.

Once the program is fully developed, the design begins in earnest. There are five standard phases for the project and their relative weights in terms of the architect's time are as follows:

Phase	Percentage of Architect's Time
Schematic Design	20%
Design Development	15%
Construction Documents	45%
Bidding or Negotiation	5%
Construction Contract Administration	15%

Schematic design phase. The schematic design phase will be very similar to the exercise performed in Chapter Five except in more detail. Your architect will prepare sketch plans of the house on the site, elevation studies, proposed materials, and usually a three-dimensional model to help you understand exactly how the house looks and works. A probable construction cost will be discussed at this time, along with its implications.

Your ideas and comprehension of the presented materials are very important at this phase. You will go through an unlimited series of revisions of the plan and investigations of various options and alternatives until you are totally satisfied with the design.

Design development phase. Once a conceptual design is approved by you, the design development phase begins. In this phase, your architect will refine each plan and elevation into more detail. Cross-sectional drawings of the house will be prepared to enable more complete coordination and understanding of the spaces. Various details will be studied and designed with respect to cost and the overall design concept of the house. Finish materials will be further described.

The finished design development package will contain enough information for submission to an independent contractor for preliminary pricing. Decisions made at this stage are critical because as you move forward from this point, the design becomes less flexible and more costly to change.

Construction documents phase. Upon your approval of the design development drawings and the proposed price, your architect will initiate the construction documents phase. In this phase, the architect prepares the detailed and dimensioned drawings, which will be submitted to the city for a building permit and to the contractor for final pricing and construction. These drawings will be accompanied by a set of specifications, which are written descriptions of materials, finishes, installation procedures, etc., and lists of technical items and responsibilities included in the construction.

Bidding phase. Once the construction documents are complete, your architect will prepare a list of acceptable contractors for your approval. You may have your own list from other sources. After you have met and reviewed the work of the potential contractors and finalized the list, your architect will provide each contractor with a set of the construction documents for his bid. Your architect will answer the contractors' questions and make clarifications throughout the bidding period. When the final bids are received, the architect will help you evaluate them, understand what they mean and select a contractor.

Negotiation phase. Once a contractor is selected, there is usually a negotiation phase with that contractor before the contract is finally awarded. Your architect will preside at meetings between you and your contractor, in which some costly items will be identified and cut from the project and modifications will be made to other items to further reduce costs. When everyone has agreed that the project is complete and within the budget, a construction contract can be drawn up and signed. Your architect can provide typical contract forms drafted by the American Institute of Architects (AIA) and used in almost all construction projects.

Construction contract administration phase. During the construction phase of the project, your architect acts as the construction contract administrator, regularly visiting the site and observing that the construction is proceeding according to the plans and specifications. The architect will review and approve the contractor's periodic requests for payment and in general keep you informed about the work in progress. Your architect is your representative at the site and will assist in settling any disputes or misunderstandings between you and your contractor.

Architect's Fee

The service described above is called a total service. In it the architect monitors the project from start to finish and is always available to provide guidance and information to his client. For this service, the architect is usually compensated in one of four ways:

1. **Lump sum:** The architect will review your project goals and quote a fixed lump sum fee to provide the service.

2. **Percentage of construction cost:** Probably the most common method, the architect's fee is based on a certain percent of the construction cost. This method does not provide the architect with any direct incentive to reduce the construction cost and save the client money; his professional responsibility and reputation usually take precedence in this situation. In addition, keep in mind that the project budget is usually determined at the beginning of design.

3. **Hourly rate plus reimbursable expenses:** In this fee arrangement, the architect is paid for every hour expended on the job at agreed rates for the type of task performed. The architect may have more incentive to maintain a lower construction cost, but the client will not know what the final fee will be until the end.

4. **Combination fee structure:** In reality, a project often starts out on an hourly basis until the extent of the work is better defined, and then the compensation switches over to percentage or lump sum for the last four segments of the service. As stated earlier, it may be beneficial to you to contract the design phase on an hourly basis since your own investigations should make this phase flow more smoothly than your architect may anticipate. An architect is always happy to make this arrangement because the design phase is usually a long and diffi-

cult time and is hard to price. Working on an hourly basis in this phase guarantees him that all his hours are covered. It also allows you to save money if you can communicate more accurately and use his time more efficiently.

The total fee for the above service will probably vary widely among the architects you interview, depending on how much experience they have, how well established they are, and how badly they want to do your project. In general, an experienced architect with an established office would require between 12 percent and 18 percent of the construction price or between $33,000 and $50,000 to provide total service on a $275,000 custom home. You can find these architects by contacting the local chapter of the AIA and requesting a list of residential design offices.

Another architect who might be just as experienced but works alone with minimal overhead may be able to provide an equal or better service for as little as $15,000. Usually this type of architect will be doing all of the work himself, rather than relaying your communications to a junior architect employee who may not completely understand or may have aspirations of his own about the design. To find an independent architect like this, call the local chapter of the AIA and ask for a list of residential architects with one- or two-man offices, or ask the home builders you interview to recommend one.

In either case, the fee could be reduced further by reducing the amount of service rendered. Usually this is done by arranging an hourly fee for design; setting a fixed fee for the design development, construction documents, bidding and negotiation phases; and agreeing to utilize the architect's time, compensated on an hourly basis, as needed during the construction phase. This can result in an overall reduction in quality standards since the architect will not be able to regularly check on progress and may result in the same amount of fee spent if a problem develops that could have been avoided with continuous observation.

Quality of Documentation

An architect's documentation for the construction set of drawings will usually be more thorough and comprehensive than the minimum required by the city inspection department or the contractor. It will contain all the required drawings plus many others describing details like window frames, stair rails, tile patterns and molding shapes that are often left to the contractor's imagination. This is good in that you will have better control over the finished project; however, a contractor will sometimes raise his price if he has to actually read the plans and detail those items in a different manner than he is accustomed. Also, if he feels an architect will be inspecting his work, he may think he will have to do a more thorough job than his usual one and may bid a higher price in anticipation of a higher quality job.

RESIDENTIAL DESIGNER

A residential designer is a person who has not passed the architectural exam given by the state, but nevertheless is a professional specializing in house design, very often in a particular style of house design. Some states have an Association of Residential Designers which may certify their own members and provide them with a stamp that simulates the architect's seal, but with no legal meaning.

Residential Designer Service

The service rendered by a residential designer is usually a very streamlined version of the service you would get from an architect.

You will be able to present your scrapbook and list of wants and needs. Usually, you will be assisted in filling out a form that will describe the basic features, rooms, etc., of your house, delving more into the physical aspects, rather than the emotional needs. Quite often a client goes to a particular residential designer because he has seen and likes the designer's style of house. In a situation such as this, the emotional aspects may already be addressed by that preview.

The residential designer will take your information and prepare a schematic design similar to that of an architect, but somewhat less complete: Usually floor plans and front elevation are provided without side or rear elevations or a three-dimensional model. You will be able to make as many revisions as you like because the schematic design

work is usually done on an hourly basis of direct time spent by the designer.

Once the schematic design is approved, the residential designer will in essence skip the design development stage and move directly into the construction documents. This can be done effectively because he will utilize the same details and style in every house and does not need to investigate any new or custom details. Usually these details are copied onto plastic film and adhered to the sheets of your plans. Any changes you make after the beginning of construction documentation will be charged on an hourly basis and added to the lump sum fee.

When the construction documents are completed, the prints are turned over to you to bid or negotiate as you will. The designer will provide you with the names of competent builders, but that is the extent of the service in this phase. Any changes you might want to make as a result of your negotiations with your contractor will be recorded as a handwritten note on your contract. Otherwise you will have to pay extra to have the designer change your plans to reflect the changes you have negotiated.

The residential designer rarely has any role in the construction stage but may agree to inspect your construction if compensated on an hourly basis.

Residential Designer's Fee

The residential designer's fee is structured to appeal to those clients who want a relatively expensive custom house, but do not want to spend much money on the design or plans. In general, there are three components of the fee structure:

1. Schematic design: All design time, including client meetings, is done on an hourly basis at approximately $50/hour.

2. Construction documents: A builder set of construction documents (minimum required drawings) will be prepared on a square-foot fee, usually around $1/square foot of house, including engineering drawings.

3. Miscellaneous services: Any changes, revisions, site visits, bidding meetings, etc., will be compensated on an hourly basis.

The above formula can produce an inexpensive set of plans if you can adhere to the system, do not investigate too many options, and do not make too many revisions to the original design or to the construction documents. The average price for this service usually comes in around $8,000.

A residential designer's fee structure can perhaps save you some money, but it may make a client more anxious about requesting changes or investigating different ideas and, therefore, less comfortable with the final design.

A builder set of drawings will get you a building permit and a construction price, but you will have very little control over what gets built and how it gets built. It becomes very important to select a contractor with strong ethical standards and good taste.

On the other hand, it often seems that clients investigate many different ideas and finally "arrive again at the place of their beginnings." The main difference may be in the satisfaction that comes with knowing that you have thoroughly examined the question. You must merely decide what the knowing is worth.

MOONLIGHT ARCHITECT

Probably the best deal for imaginative design at the lowest rates is to find a youngish architect who works for an architectural firm, but would agree to do your project on an after-hours or "moonlight" basis.

Since architectural offices are notorious for how little they pay their employees, most firms allow their junior employees to make extra money in this manner. Most young architects will jump at the opportunity to design a project on their own since they feel constantly frustrated carrying out the bosses' orders.

The trick is finding the right young architect for your project. Architects who are too young will tend to be headstrong and too flamboyant in their designs and may not have enough residential construction experience, and residential construction is very different from commercial construction. Architects who are too old will probably be partners in the firm and are expected to bring their jobs into the office. Ideally, you should try to find someone in his early thirties who works for or has worked for an office that specializes in residential design. This may not be as hard as it sounds.

Everyone knows an architect or has a cousin who is one. Ask around and follow one lead into another until you find the right person. You will have to schedule your project around his real job, but most clients prefer to meet in the evenings anyway. Of course, the drawings will take longer to complete, but it is a chance to save several thousand dollars on the fee.

HOME BUILDER DRAFTING SERVICE

Most residential contractors have a residential designer or draftsman that they work with on an ongoing basis. If you have a set of plans that need only minor modifications, this type of service should suffice. A minor hourly rate between $15/hour and $25/hour can be expected.

DRAFTSMAN

An ordinary draftsman may be able to produce the proper drawings for a permit, depending upon the type of drafting experience he has. Again, this might be a value if you know exactly what you want and don't particularly care how it is done. The key to this option would be to find a draftsman that works in an architect's or designer's office who would be willing to moonlight your job for a greatly reduced fee. Most of these draftsmen are willing and eager to perform this service, but timing could become somewhat problematic since their hours are limited by their other jobs.

ARCHITECTURAL STUDENT

Some fifth-year architectual students who have had some experience working in residential design offices may be able to provide a suitable design and drawing service at a very reasonable price.

I list the architectural students here in order to cover all the options. I do not doubt their qualifications to provide an interesting and perhaps good schematic design, but your house is a large and important project, and in construction there is absolutely no substitute for experience.

CHAPTER SIX REVIEW

Types of professional designers: Definitions and discussion of six types of designers.

Services to expect from each type: The different levels of services to expect from each type of designer.

Fee ranges: The typical fee structures and price ranges for the different design professionals.

Advantages and disadvantages of each type: The pros and cons of each type of designer and suggested ways to arrange your contract to save you money on your designer.

CHAPTER 7

FINDING AND SELECTING YOUR DESIGN PROFESSIONAL

> **In this chapter, we will cover:**
>
> ✔ Finding candidates to interview ✔ References
> ✔ Questions for the interview ✔ Evaluation of the interview
> ✔ Viewing the work

I n order to find the right design professional for your specific project parameters, it may be necessary and informative to interview several candidates in different categories. The first step in this process is to make a list of possible candidates.

FINDING CANDIDATES TO INTERVIEW

Although most architects are capable of and willing to design within the vocabularies of many different styles, if you can organize your list around architects who have designed and built projects you like, you are one step ahead of the game. Drive around neighborhoods that have residential projects under way or newly completed. When you see one you like, stop and ask who designed the project. Most projects under construction will have the designer's name on a construction sign near the road.

Another good way to find the right designer is to ask friends, colleagues and acquaintances if they know or can recommend an architect or designer. If that referred person happens to be a commercial architect, all the better, because he will usually know several residential design colleagues in different price categories whom he can personally recommend to you.

Many times, a prospective new home client has already opened a dialogue with a builder before he has located his designer. Any builder will usually be able to refer you to several architects and residential designers whom he has worked with or has

heard about and give you some idea of their specialty and price.

If you are interested in talking to an architect, and you should definitely consider at least interviewing some architects, you can call the local chapter of the American Institute of Architects and give a description of the type of architect you think you need. The AIA will provide you with a list of referrals free of charge, and no one will call you if you choose not to pursue the matter.

Most areas have a regional home-building show several times a year, where builders and designers have booths set up to display their wares and meet prospective clients. This would be a good place to locate residential designers, but probably not many architects.

Lastly, you can just let your fingers do the walking and consult the yellow pages. Residential designers can be found under that heading or under "Designers, Residential." For architects, you can pick any firm, and tell the receptionist you would like to speak to an architect for some general information. Almost any architect will be happy to spend a few minutes on the phone with you to answer your questions and to recommend another architect who specializes in residential design if he does not.

After some amount of investigation, narrow your list of candidates down to three to five names. Call them and request interviews, either at your site or their offices. If you meet at your site, you may get some free and exciting advice about what you should build. If you go to their offices, you will have the opportunity to see their operations for yourself and can gain more insight into them and into their projects.

IMPORTANT QUESTIONS FOR THE INTERVIEW

During the interview, you must try to gather as much information as possible about the designer, his experience, his firm's history, the services available and fees. It's also important that you feel comfortable with the individual(s) with whom you'll work. The questions listed here will help you gather this information.

How Large Is the Firm and How Long in Practice?

In general, the larger firms have more overhead and must charge more for their services. The principal architect, around whom the firm is centered, may be famous, but he will probably not be able to give your project his complete attention. He will probably do some conceptual sketches in your meetings and oversee the work, but he will not do the actual drawings. If his firm is managed well, the junior architect who will handle your job will be experienced and knowledgeable about his boss's architectural vocabulary, and you will be able to deal directly with him when his boss is unavailable.

The worst case scenario is that you may get shoved off onto a junior designer with little experience. The principal architect may only see your plans minutes before each meeting with you and may not be successfully communicating your instructions to his assistants. If this is the case, you will be able to sense that you are not getting a proper service, and let them know this in writing. This may create a little tension for a while, but should solve the problem.

Large projects require many architects working together to produce the work in a timely manner. Residential projects are comparatively small but complicated and cannot stand too many hands stirring the pot. If you choose a small firm or one-man office, you know that the man in the meeting is also directly involved in producing the work and that

your comments and concerns will not be lost in the communication void. Further, since your designer is directly involved in producing the work, he will tend to care more about the quality and design of your project because he has a greater time investment in it. Many architects and designers do not want to have a large office because they will have to become managers instead of designers. Much of the best residential work will come out of small, manageable firms in which the principal architect has direct involvement in the day-to-day design decisions.

Firms that have been in practice longer will be better known and will have more work than newer firms that have not yet had enough time to build a reputation. Architectural firms that have plenty of work will charge a higher fee than those that need the next job. If you have a great concern about the fee, look for the small, newer firms that are run by an older experienced designer. He may have been managing that larger firm last year. Also, firms with more history may appear more stable, but it is unlikely you will be building another house anytime soon.

Ask to See Examples of Projects Similar to Your Own

Any architect or designer will expect to show you his portfolio of work. If the discussions seem serious, the candidate will offer to take you through private homes he has designed, and you can "feel" the spaces and observe firsthand how he and his former clients interacted. Any good designer can work with your ideas of style or architectural character. When you visit one of his homes, look for more abstract qualities such as grace, proportion, taste, warmth, livability and sensitivity. These qualities are what make a house a home and are the most difficult goals for the designer to achieve.

Who Will Be Doing the Actual Work in Each Phase?

As mentioned above, your project will probably have several people involved in the various phases. Ask to meet all of these people, and try to determine if you will be able to like them personally. This is very important in a residential project, and you have a right to work with people you can respect and admire.

Ask for a Complete Breakdown of the Extent of the Service

Your architect will be glad to explain the details of his service if you ask. Use the following questions to open a dialogue about what will be provided in each phase.

Schematic design: How many alternates will you see at the first presentation? What kind of drawings will you see at the first presentation? Will there be a model? How many revisions can be made? How are fees determined and charged in this phase? Will there be charges for excessive revisions?

Design development: What will be my (the client's) involvement in this phase? How will changes and revisions be handled in this phase? Will there be extra charges?

Construction documentation: How will minor changes be handled in this phase? Will there be extra charges? What about major changes in this phase?

Bidding and negotiations: What assistance is provided in this phase for putting the drawings out to bid? In negotiations with the contractor, will the drawings and specifications be revised to reflect the bid negotiations? Will there be extra charges?

Construction contract administration: What service, if any, is included for this phase? Approximately how many site visits are included? Who in the firm will be responsible for this phase? Will they be available to answer questions from the contractor and from the client?

How Much Will It Cost?

Do not be shy about asking about the price of the service. Many fee structures are set up such that design is done on an hourly basis because a designer cannot predict how difficult it will be to please a particular client or how well the client will be able to stand by his own decisions. Even so, the designer should be able to give you a good idea of the average schematic design cost for a house similar to your own, as well as a maximum price for the schematic design phase.

The other phases are much easier to price because they are more predictable. Any detail you see for the first time should come with a free modification or revision. Revisions resulting from a client's change of mind or new directions are sometimes charged on an hourly basis since they are out of a designer's control.

The so-called bargain design fees are very sensitive to extra time spent and usually come with strict rules about revisions and extra work being directly compensated. These fees may seem low at the beginning, but by the end the client has often had to pay considerably more that he expected to and has that bad feeling that he has been nickeled-and-dimed to death.

On the other hand, if a designer has negotiated a good fee from the beginning, he usually does not worry too much about revisions, extra work or new directions because he has already accounted for a certain amount of that in his fee, and it is more important to maintain a good, friendly working relationship with the client than to account for every minute of the job.

How Busy Is the Firm at Present?

Almost anyone will tell you with great pride that he is very busy in his work if he is. It seems like most people will tell you the same thing even if they aren't. Still, make an attempt to find out how much work the firm has now and in the immediate future. If the firm is very busy, ask how it will work your job into the workload and how long to expect it to take for the completion of the schematic design phase and the construction documents. Ask for a tentative schedule of meetings to review the above work.

Do You Have a Favorable Impression of the Person?

Although the discussion above has been about the extent of service and the price, the most important point by far in the selection of your designer is how well you like him, which will impact how well you will be able to work with him. The questions for your interview will tell you much about the process and help define exactly what service you can expect, but these points can be listed in a brochure or contract. The real point of the interview is to develop a feeling about the person and to decide if it is a favorable one.

Ask for References and Phone Numbers

Another good measure for your designer is how well he rates with previous clients. Ask for a list of recent clients and their phone numbers and actually call them for their reference. The architect/client relationship becomes very intense, almost like family, during the project, and if the previous client is cool or noncommittal about his designer, be concerned. Remember, some clients are tough cookies, but still be concerned. Also ask if the designer was responsible in returning calls, being on time for meetings, etc., as constant tardiness or failure to return calls can become very frustrating in a project.

EVALUATING THE CANDIDATES

When you have finished the interview period, try to evaluate each candidate objectively and unemotionally. Use the following questions to help you in your evaluation.

Did the Designer Seem to Be Interested in Your Project?

Obviously, it is fairly easy to fake interest in a prospective new project. However, if the designer seemed arrogant or oblivious to you and your project, he is probably not the designer for you.

Did You Like the Designer's Previous Projects?

Did the projects you were shown have any special charm or remarkable quality, or did they appear to be the standard competent job? Did the spaces in the house appear to be ones in which you would feel comfortable? Was there anything exciting or interesting in the work? Did the designer express any excitement when describing his work to you?

How Do the Prices Compare?

In design services in general, one tends to get the service one pays for. There are many exceptions in which an architect or designer may provide a more complete service than that for which he is being compensated because he simply wants to do a good job and hopes that a good job here will lead to a

better job in the future. This is a relatively common situation, but still not one to depend upon because that designer is often understaffed and overextended; his interest in his designs hinders his business skills.

The best advice for a client is to decide what level of service he wants and can afford, and compare the prices from the different design professionals who provide that type of service.

Did the Designer Listen Carefully to Your Needs?

Of course, in an interview, a designer is expected to tell the interviewer everything about his firm and answer any other reasonable questions he is asked. However, if you came away with the impression that your designer was only interested in talking about himself and did not really listen to you or your needs, he may not be the one for you.

Did the Designer Make You Feel Comfortable?

Again, this question comes back to the overriding issue of personal attraction. Did you feel that the designer was "speaking your language" and that you could communicate easily with him? If he was speaking arrogantly, talking over your head, or in any other way intimidating to you, keep looking for a more comfortable consultant.

Did You Like the Designer Personally?

I keep coming back to this issue because it is really the most important one to consider. Assuming all the designers on your short list have about the same level of experience and are offering the same level of service, the only other important items are quality of design and your communication level. Since design quality is a completely subjective issue and we assume he is on your short list because you like his work, the only outstanding point, and indeed the major point, is the communication between client and designer.

It is very important that you select a designer you would like for a brother-in-law or sister-in-law because you need to develop a close relationship with that person during this time, and that can only happen if the chemistry is right.

Does the Designer Seem Responsible?

Did you get the feeling that this person will return your call no matter how bad the news? Will he be where he said he would be at the agreed time? These are situations in a project that can be very frustrating if they become repetitive. Ask your references about this and make up your own mind.

At the end of your interview period, you will have a strong idea of which professional you want to use. Remember that the relationship between architect and client is a very intense one, so be certain to pick someone who can communicate with you and with whom you want to spend a great deal of time.

CHAPTER SEVEN REVIEW

Finding candidates to interview: How to locate the designers you want to interview.

Questions for the interview: Example questions for a thorough interview and explanations of what to look for in the answers.

Viewing the work: What to look for in the work of the designers to tell you if they are right for you.

References: Sample questions to ask previous clients and what to look for in the answers.

Evaluation of the interview: The bottom line of the interview process.

CHAPTER 8

YOUR CONTRACTOR AND OTHER PROFESSIONALS

In this chapter, we will cover:

✔ Soils engineer
✔ Structural engineer
✔ Mechanical, electrical and plumbing engineer

✔ General contractor
✔ General contactor interview
✔ Evaluation of the interview

There are a number of other professionals who should or will be involved in your project along with your designer. Some of them are listed below with a brief description of what they will do.

SOILS ENGINEER

The soils engineer is a specialist in analyzing the subsurface conditions under your foundation. This person's responsibility is to take samples from your site, test and evaluate them, and make recommendations for your foundation type. He will come to your site and drill two to three holes in the ground at your proposed building location. Sample material from each test hole will be taken back to the laboratory for various tests. Finally, a report will be published describing such things as the soil conditions, the best foundation for your structure, safe bearing values of the soil, and proper depths for footings.

Many cities will require that this soils investigation be performed before the building foundation is designed. Required or not, it is always a good idea. Your designer can recommend a soils engineer, or you can find one in the yellow pages under "Engineers, Soils." The total fee for the field work, testing and report is about $600—well worth the cost when you consider how important your foundation will be and how much money you will spend on top of it.

STRUCTURAL ENGINEER

Many cities will also require a structural engineer to design and seal your foundation. The structural engineer will work directly with your designer or architect to calculate design loadings and prepare a foundation design as recommended by your soils report. The cost for this service will be about $300-$500.

The structural engineer can also design the aboveground wood and/or steel structural frame for your project, including joist and decking sizes. The cost for this service is again around $300-$500. Your architect or designer may do the framing plan himself (and charge you for it). Ask him if the structural design is included in his fee, and if so, how much will he reduce the fee if you request a structural engineer to provide the foundation and structural design and drawings. Again, you are not talking about much money to get a more expert service provided on a very important part of your project.

MECHANICAL, ELECTRICAL AND PLUMBING ENGINEER

Generally on houses, the mechanical, electrical and plumbing (MEP) drawings are provided by the respective subcontractors. MEP engineering is very expensive and few home builders want to spend that extra money on engineering fees. Most important items in these categories can be covered satisfactorily in the specifications. Your designer should furnish a schematic diagram showing the air handler locations and how the duct work is threaded through the structure. Major plumbing risers should also be identified within the structure. Your subcontractors will then refer to these schematic diagrams when laying out the physical system in the field.

GENERAL CONTRACTOR

The most important professional involved in your project (other than your architect or designer) will be your general contractor. This person should be selected with the same care and caution with which you selected your architect or designer, following an interview period and competitive bidding.

You can make a list of potential candidates by driving around your new neighborhood and taking names off the job signs in front of new construction sites. This method assures you that they are familiar with the local ordinances and are building for prices similar to the ones for which you are looking.

Again, friends or colleagues are always good for referrals. Your architect or designer will be well acquainted with several general contractors within your price range and will be best able to evaluate them in terms of price, quality and performance.

Home builder shows are good places to meet residential general contractors and to see photographs of their work. Often, your neighborhood group or subdivision office will have a list of acceptable general contractors and subcontractors who have experience doing work in the community.

Before you set up interviews with any potential general contractors, there are a few things you should know about the deal.

The General Contractor's Deal

The general contractor is the knowledgeable, experienced person who will be responsible for the construction of your project. A general contractor's license is required in some states, but his experience record should be reviewed by your bank and approved before you sign a contract. He should also be required to furnish proof of "builder's risk" insurance for your project, which will pay to have the project finished if some unfortunate circumstance prohibits the general contractor from completing the job.

The general contractor will take your finished construction documents and specifications and request bids from each trade or subcontractor needed for the job, usually subcontractors he uses on a regular basis. Most of the time the owner has no voice in which subcontractors are hired or how much they are paid. These subcontractors are independent businessmen who are taking their own risks on their price for their part of your job and are not in the direct employ of the general contractor. Many of your subcontractors, such as electrical, mechanical and plumbing, will be required to be licensed by the state.

When the general contractor receives the bids from the subcontractors, he adds them up. To this subtotal, he adds a figure (usually a percentage of the whole) for his "overhead and profit." The subcontract totals plus his overhead and profit is the cost of construction of your project.

The general contractor's fee is referred to as his cost for his overhead and profit on the job. The typical general contractor's business overhead consists of a small office with a secretary/bookkeeper/receptionist employee, a pickup truck, a beeper and a car phone. His job overhead may include temporary power to the site, a job telephone, and possibly a superintendent.

The typical general contractor's overhead and profit ranges from 15 percent to 20 percent of the total job cost. His job is to organize your project, hire the subcontractors, schedule the work, supervise the overall construction, assume the responsibility for the work and to assign that responsibility to the various subs, solve the problems and complete the job. Actual overhead will be a very small part of the overhead and profit item, but it sounds better than just profit.

The general contractor will usually have as many jobs going at one time as he can handle (or more than he can handle), which will greatly impact how much time he will spend at your site and how much attention he can give your project.

He will make a request for payment (a draw) every month to cover all labor and materials installed in the job in the preceding month. After an inspection of the job and approval of the amount by your architect or bank's inspector, the general contractor should be paid 90 percent of his request from the construction account. The 10 percent held back is called retainage or retention, and its purpose is to maintain the contractor's interest level in your job when other wheels are squeaking louder than yours. Retainage is standard practice in commercial construction and is the only real leverage you may have on your general when you need his attention. Understandably, residential contractors do not like the idea of retainage, but it will keep you where you need to be on your job—in control.

In many states, a subcontractor's lien may be paid off with the 10 percent retainage even if the sub has received no money from the general. Retainage is also required by most banks that provide interim financing. If your general contractor balks at retainage, check your local ordinances and your bank, and then consider another contractor.

At the stage of "substantial completion" of the job, just before the contractor is ready to turn the project over to the owner and when the contractor has given the owner signed lien waivers from each subcontractor, the contractor may be paid half of the outstanding retainage. Another half of the remaining sum may be paid at the completion of the "final punch list" (the list of outstanding items yet to be completed or accepted), but some amount should be held until you have occupied the house for thirty days and the "final, final punch list" has been completed.

The General Contractor Interview

In any event, after you have prepared a list of candidates, you will definitely want to schedule a personal interview and visit a number of their finished projects before you put their name on your bid list. Some important questions and discussion topics for the interview are listed and explained below.

1. How long have you been in business? Residential general contracting is a business in which experience counts. Some states require that a general contractor be registered and licensed by the state, but many do not. It is important that your general contractor has many years of personal experience in the business as it is fraught with problems. It is also important that his contracting business has been around for a long period of time as

this proves that he has managed his resources well. Because there are great risks in the business, many of the careless residential contractors are in and out of personal bankruptcy all the time. It could save you some headaches to avoid contractors with such a history.

This can be done by requesting bank references, a relatively standard procedure. If a contractor continues to ignore your request for recent banking history, be concerned.

2. How many projects do you currently have under way? At what stages of construction are they? How large is your company? The number of projects on any contractor's plate at one time is important in several ways. A contractor's price may vary greatly with respect to how badly he needs the job. If he is busy for the near future, your job may be one that he could do without unless he can make a larger than average profit on it. Unless you are willing to pay a premium for a particular contractor, you may want to pass if he is loaded with work.

If some projects are in the final stages of construction, they may be finished by the time yours comes on line. If most of the projects are in the early stages, ask how much of his time will be available to you and your job.

Although many do very large projects, most residential contractors have very small companies, usually consisting of the contractor and a bookkeeper/telephone answering person. If a contractor has more than three jobs under construction that are not yet halfway finished, he may not be able to stretch himself far enough to give you the service you deserve. Ask him how many superintendents he employs and how many hours per day either he or a superintendent will be on your site.

3. Will there be a full-time superintendent on site? A full-time superintendent would be on site all day to guide the work, interpret the plans, and solve the problems for the subcontractors as they arise. Few residential projects have the budgets that can afford to pay a full-time site superintendent, but it is a point that needs to be clarified up front.

Without a full-time superintendent, mistakes will be picked up after they are constructed, if at all. This will place a heavier burden on the owner and his designer to carefully check the work often, because the farther along the construction goes before a mistake is discovered, the more costly it will be to make it right. If the owner or his architect do not discover the mistake, a contractor may fix it anyway, or he may make other changes in the work to accommodate it.

It is the general contractor's responsibility to build the project according to the plans, and if a mistake is made, he should fix it. If there is no architect involved in construction administration, the owner must have the resolve to stand firmly on this issue, even though the contractor may feel it is unreasonable.

4. Discuss the fee arrangement you are expecting on your job. There are three basic fee arrangements most commonly used in residential construction:

A) **Percentage of total cost:** This fee structure is the most common. The contractor's compensation (overhead and profit) is reflected in his price as a percentage added to the total of the material's price and the subcontractors' labor prices. Under this arrangement, if the contractor were to save you money on the job, the savings would erode his own profit.

B) **Lump sum fee:** This fee is a specified amount to be paid to the general contractor for completing the job and is independent of the total project cost. This fee arrangement allows the contractor to save you money without reducing his own fee. Often times, this arrangement includes a fifty-fifty split of any savings below the maximum price if the contractor can bring the job in for a lower price. This is the only arrangement that gives the contractor real incentive to keep costs down.

C) **Hourly with a guaranteed maximum:** In this arrangement, the contractor would be compensated at an agreed hourly rate, with a maximum price guaranteed for the total cost of the project. As above, a fifty-fifty split of any savings below the maximum price can be utilized to everyone's benefit.

5. Insist upon open accounting. Most general contractors will agree to show you the actual invoices for the various trades and materials on the jobs after the bid and later as they come in during construction. This practice may not eliminate kickbacks from the subcontractor to the general, but at least it makes them more complicated.

6. Ask to visit recent projects. All contractors will be proud to show off their work. What you see is the quality of work you can expect for the price being quoted. Take the time to acquaint yourself with each contractor's projects.

7. Ask for references and telephone numbers. Just as with your designer, recent client references are very important in selecting your contractor. Ask the former client the following questions:

A) How were changes and revisions handled?
B) Were minor changes charged?
C) How much time did the contractor spend on the job each day?
D) How much difficulty to get sloppy work redone?
E) Was the job completed on time?
F) Was the contractor always accessible?
G) Are you happy with the finished product?
H) Would you hire him again?

8. Ask for architect references. Even though previous clients may have been happy with the performance of the general contractor, they are not really able to judge his technical competence or knowledge and won't be able to judge it until the wood window sills begin rotting away in a few years. Ask your candidate if he has built houses with any architects and ask for the architects' names. These professionals will be able to give you an idea of the contractor's technical skills and should be happy to do so. Many of these architects may even offer construction services and can be hired by the hour to come to your site and give an opinion on a questionable detail or problem.

9. Are you agreeable to 10 percent retainage? As stated before, this is not only the law in some states, it is the only real leverage you will have to get the contractor to finish the last little bits and pieces of the job when his attention has moved on to other jobs. Many residential contractors will tell you they never do retainage, but if you insist, they will usually come around. Also, if after repeated delays you finally have to hire someone to finish the work, you can deduct that cost from the retainage you still owe your general contractor. If you have no retainage, you are out the money and out of luck.

10. Discuss no monies down. Some contractors will request a down payment or advance to start the construction, with offers to repay the money by deducting it from the first few draws. A good rule of thumb is to never let your contractor get ahead of you financially. If your contractor does not have the credit to purchase materials to start the job, you might question his financial depth. Money should be released to the contractor only for materials and labor already used on the job, and keep the retainage on those payments.

Evaluating the Candidates

After you have visited previous jobs and interviewed a few contractors, you will feel that you know a great deal more about the home building business. Before you make your selection for bidders on your job, ask yourself these questions:

Were you satisified with the quality of craftsmanship on the jobs you visited? The architectural design and/or the interior design of his projects may not be the contractor's fault, but bad craftsmanship probably is. Look for cracks in the sheet rock above the doors and windows on the interior and cracks in the brick mortar joints at the same place on the exterior. Look for cracks in the driveway, garage slab or sidewalk. Look for stains from water leaks around the windows. Look for lighting fixtures or plumbing fixtures that are not precisely mounted. Look for changes in the floor level when the floor material changes. Most of all, look for cracks or spaces in the trim work and finish carpentry around windows, doors and cabinets.

How do his prices compare to those of the other candidates? There are many levels of residential contractors available to build any job. Price is almost always related to quality; however, most contractors will try to fix poor craftsmanship problems if you or your architect demands a better job. The biggest problem you may have in this area is knowing what quality you can reasonably demand.

Better contractors will need much less supervision in this area because they have the knowledge and the budget to do a better job without being told. A higher price may mean a better contractor, or it may only mean that a particular contractor has plenty of work in the foreseeable future and can afford to lose your job. You will need to decide this in each case.

Your project visits should tell you something about quality, and you should not try to compare two contractors' prices without taking their quality standards into account. Also realize that you will need to do much more supervision to get the same quality job from a cheaper contractor.

Does he seem responsible? Take notice if your contractor candidate is habitually late or misses meetings. Ask his references about his sense of responsibility. Working with a contractor who cannot be on time can be very frustrating.

Do you like him personally? It may seem like a strange criterion for a business decision, but it may be the most important question you will ask yourself about your contractor. If he seems like the sort of person you might like as a friend, you will probably be friends on the job and will be able to work problems out more effectively. If his manner is brusque or he rubs you the wrong way, six to eight months of exposure and tribulations will only make matters worse.

Do you trust him? Does his manner inspire the trust and confidence that he will deal fairly with you through the project? Will he open his bid account book and show you bids or invoices for materials? Or does he seem to be manipulating numbers or obscuring your understanding of them? Does he seem like a used car salesman or a gentleman? Again, if he seems a little slimy at the offset, it is not very likely to get any better five months into the job.

Remember, you will be spending a lot of time with your contractor, and you must work very closely with him throughout the project. It will be important to like, respect and trust him because there will be times of tension in every project. If your designer or architect is involved in the construction phase, he can help work out the differences as your agent and knowledgeable third party. If you do not have this service from your designer, it becomes of critical importance to select the right contractor for the project.

You and your contractor should work as a team to solve the many problems that invariably arise. If the mutual respect and trust between contractor and owner are lost, your teamwork may be replaced by a feeling of antagonism, which can often lead to emotional threats of legal action. This situation should be monitored closely and avoided if at all possible. Withholding payments can easily lead to a lien on your property title, which will be expensive to remove regardless of who is right. Other lawsuits can be continuously postponed and drag out for years, benefiting only the lawyers in the end.

If you begin to feel uncomfortable with your relationship with your contractor, ask your architect or designer to mediate the problems with the job. He will know more than you about the technical issues of the problem and can usually convince the contractor to do the right thing. Above all else, keep a cool head and remember that you and your contractor are both working toward the same goal—completing a project of which you can both be proud.

CHAPTER EIGHT REVIEW

Other professionals: Descriptions of the other professionals involved in your job, what they will do for you, and how much it should cost.

General contractor: An explanation of the general contractor's job description and his remuneration.

General contractor interview: A list of questions to help you find out what you need to know about your candidates in order to make the right choice.

Evaluation of the interview: Answers to the questions and a discussion of what to look for in the projects you visit to determine the true quality of the contractor's work.

CHAPTER 9

SUBCONTRACTORS

In this chapter, we will cover:

✔ *Subcontractors' titles and responsibilities*

The people who will actually build your house are the subcontractors and their crews. Your general contractor is responsible for organizing the work, but the subs (for short) are the independent craftsmen and tradesmen who actually do the physical work. The subs, who are not employees of the general contractor, are hired by the job and often work only for one or two general contractors if they can generate enough work to keep them busy.

You may never actually meet most of your subcontractors, but many, such as your framing contractor, will probably become very familiar to you. Know them or not, it is a good idea to know what they are doing on your job.

Grading Contractor

Your grading contractor will do all the earthwork on your site, including excavation, filling and finish contouring (grading). He is usually the first on the site unless an existing building has been demolished. This contractor will first "shoot the grades" of your site, so you can determine how high you want to place the top of your foundation and which direction the site will eventually drain. He will then subtract the depth of your basement (if any), the thickness of your concrete slab and whatever thickness of fill material is required under your slab, and grade the building site down to that level. The topsoil (upper twelve inches) should always be removed and, if possible, be saved for finish grading

if there is an area for storing it on your site.

Suitable fill material will then be trucked in and dumped on your building site. The grading contractor will then grade the fill in "lifts" (six- to ten-inch increments) and compact each layer as he goes. Final grading should accommodate any drops or slopes in the slab above since the slab thickness should be constant.

After the foundation fill is graded, the grading contractor goes away until the end of the job. He will return to grade the driveway and sidewalk slabs, and when the house is almost finished, he will do the final grading of the site. This should include replacing topsoil, sloping all grade away from your house, and sloping the yard in such a manner that it will drain toward the city street or alley and away from your site.

Foundation Contractor

The foundation contractor will excavate and place all foundations below the surface of the site. This will include drilled piers with bell-bottoms (the footings for your foundation slab) and basement or retaining wall footings.

These footings are usually concrete and will have exposed steel (reinforcing) bars sticking out of the tops. These bars will be tied into the steel in your surface concrete when it is poured later.

Concrete Contractor

The concrete contractor will do the trenching and formwork required to pour your concrete slab. He will place the steel reinforcing bars in the beam trenches and in the slab, and pour, level and finish your concrete slabs.

Plumbing Contractor

Your plumbing contractor will design the plumbing runs and risers for your house and will work in conjunction with the concrete contractor to trench and place the required drainpipes under the slab before it is poured. After the framing is complete, the plumbing contractor will return and run supply, drain and vent piping throughout the house. He will return once again near the end of the job to install your plumbing fixtures and hardware.

Electrical Contractor

Your electrical contractor will design the electrical circuitry for your house according to the loads specified by the plans. He will make the connection to the city power drop, place your meter and breaker box, install all wiring through the frame, and return later to install outlets, switches and cover plates.

Framing Contractor

The framing contractor will erect the structural frame of your house, including walls, columns, beams, joists, rafters, floor and roof decking. He will usually install the windows, exterior sheathing, moisture membrane on the exterior of the house, and any exterior wood siding.

Roofing Contractor

The roofing contractor will install your roof system, complete with metal flashing (strips of galvanized metal placed at the edges of your roof), vent boots (metal flashing around vent pipes) and rain gutters.

Masonry Contractor

The masonry contractor will lay the brick veneer on the exterior of the house, if any.

Insulation Contractor

The insulation contractor will provide and install all insulation materials in your walls, floors and attics.

Drywall Contractor

This subcontractor will hang the Sheetrock on the interior walls and ceilings of your house, tape and float the joints, and texture the finish in preparation for painting.

Ironwork Contractor

This contractor will provide and install any steelwork needed for your job, such as beam seats, steel columns, metal stair rails or balcony rails.

Millwork Contractor

The millwork contractor will build and install all the cabinetwork in your house.

Finish and Trim Contractor

This highly skilled finish carpenter will do all the carpentry work that is exposed to view. He will usually hang doors, trim doors and windows, trim cabinets, install baseboards, etc. He may even build and/or hang the cabinets.

Flooring Contractor

Different flooring contractors will install the different flooring systems as required, including carpet, wood floors, tile floors, etc.

Tile Contractor

The tile contractor will install bathroom ceramic tile, kitchen quarry tiles, etc.

Painting Contractor

Your painting contractor will be responsible for painting the interior and exterior of your house.

Mechanical (HVAC) Contractor

The mechanical (or HVAC) contractor will design your air conditioning and heating system to the requirements specified in your plans. He will install ducts through the structural frame, furnaces, fan units, vents and compressors. He will return toward the end of the job to install your grilles, filters, etc.

Cleanup Contractor

One cleanup contractor will come by your site from time to time to haul off trash and piles of building material scraps. Another will come at the end of the job to totally clean up the finished house, including the windows, before you move in.

Often a construction situation will arise in which some responsibilities are not clearly delegated to one particular contractor or another. In these gray areas, the general contractor is the judge and jury, but he always hopes to anticipate the situation. Recently I was on a job with some very unusual windows. I noticed that the glazing job was quite a mess, and it seemed to me that it would be much easier to clean it up before the putty hardened. I asked the glazer why he didn't clean up as he finished each window to reduce the amount of work later. He replied that he never cleaned up

after himself on a job and that it would be the general contractor's problem. That was news to the general contractor on the job. But I was sure that he could handle the problem because the window supplier had not been paid in full. I think the glazer was also in for some news soon afterwards.

CHAPTER NINE REVIEW

Subcontractors' titles and responsibilities: The typical subs you will encounter on your project and their responsibilities on your job.

UNDERSTANDING THE BIDDING PROCEDURE

In this chapter, we will cover:

- ✔ Types of bids
- ✔ Bidding procedure
- ✔ Negotiating the price
- ✔ The itemized cost sheet
- ✔ Line items
- ✔ Potential savings areas

After you have a completed set of plans, the next step will be to obtain a firm construction cost, based on the plans, from an experienced residential contractor.

Before you move into the actual bid process, it might be worth noting that the first bids on all projects come in higher than an owner ever dreamed, wanted to pay, can believe, etc. Don't worry, you are only having a typical experience. Clients always seem to ask for more than they can afford, often against the advice of their designers. Maybe they hope that in their specific case, the things they want to include in their house will be less expensive. It is seldom the case.

In fact, designing more than you can afford and then stripping the design to get it into budget is not the most efficient or best way to the end, but it will get you there eventually. And by the time it is all over, you will have a good idea of the price of each material and fixture in your house.

CONSTRUCTION PRICE

The construction price can be derived in various ways. Use the following descriptions of pricing methods to help you decide how you prefer to handle this crucial step in your home building process.

Negotiated Price From One Contractor

This method involves an ongoing relationship with a selected contractor. If you know one you trust to be fair with you, this is probably the best and easiest way to design and build the house you can afford. The contractor can be included in the design team just after the schematic plans and elevations are approved. The designer and you can then use the contractor's expertise and judgment to help make the critical decisions regarding finish materials, construction techniques, framing systems, etc. In this way, you know and can control the cost all the way through the design process. Your finished design is already priced and will contain no surprises and need no extensive changes at the end. And you can save the two- to four-week bidding time period.

Competitive Bid

In this method, you will issue a completed set of plans and specifications to a list of three to five general contractors you have selected as potential candidates for the job. They will examine the drawings with their subcontractors and return a firm price for the project in two to three weeks. Usually, the price is accompanied with a list of suggestions for substitution of materials and systems that they feel will make the project better or cheaper.

Cost Plus With Guaranteed Maximum

A cost plus contract means that the owner pays all the costs directly associated with the job (all materials and subcontractors' labor costs) plus a fee to the general contractor for managing the job. The general contractor works on your project as your employee for an hourly amount or an agreed lump sum fee as his remuneration. This arrangement removes the element of risk (mistakes, increases in materials' costs, etc.) from his position (and places it in your lap). All contractors love a cost plus contract. Unfortunately, this type of contract is somewhat open-ended in terms of completion price and offers little incentive to the contractor to save his client money.

Therefore, a variation of the agreement has been developed with a guaranteed maximum price affixed to it. This type of agreement assures the owner of the worst-case price, but still leaves little incentive for the contractor to try to bring it in lower. This incentive can be made by an offer to split any cost savings fifty-fifty with the contractor.

Negotiated Bid

The most common method for selecting the contractor is a combination of the first two methods, in which you will receive the competitive bids from three to five contractors as in a routine bidding procedure.

During this process you will have more contact with each contractor, and by the time the bids are accepted, you will have a good idea which contractors you would like to know better. Hopefully, a couple of the nicer ones will appear among the low bidders.

Select the contractor you like most who is close to your own budget figure. Try to compare his costs for individual items with costs from the other bids to check for any outstanding deviations. Then arrange a meeting with yourself, your designer, and the contractor to negotiate his price to fit your budget. Go over the plans to make certain he has understood your intent correctly. Your designer should have some ideas on areas to reduce the price. In addition, the contractor will make suggestions for material substitutions or easier ways of accomplishing your design. After a few rounds of these talks, the cost can usually be reduced to fit your budget, the drawings changed accordingly, and a contract signed.

THE INVITATION TO BID

When you have all your bid documents (drawings and specifications) in order and you have selected your bid candidates (usually three to five bids will be sufficient to cover a range of pricing and personalities), you are ready to put your project out for competitive bids.

If you have a full service design contract with an architect, the bidding will be handled by his office. If not, you will need a cover letter for each bid package. A sample bid letter is shown on page 93.

Each bid letter should be accompanied by instructions explaining the "rules" of the competition. These instructions cover all the usual questions the bidders may ask and protect the owner from liability resulting from an unhappy bidder. The bid form will also give all necessary information regarding the requirements of the bid, additional copies of plans and specifications, and specifics about addenda and questions concerning the plans or bids. A sample of typical bid instructions can be found in Appendix B.

Bid Forms

Each contractor will have a different method for organizing his subcontract bidders and grouping their prices. In order to make your analysis and comparison of the bids as easy as possible, you should provide each contractor with a standard form for his bid. This form also explains certain stipulations which will be imposed by the contract and must be agreeable to the contractor. A sample bid form can be found in Appendix B of this book.

UNDERSTANDING YOUR BIDS

When you have received your bids, your real work begins. First of all, remember what has already been said about initial prices: They are always shocking. Don't worry. Roll up your sleeves and wade into the confusion.

The next step is to select one or two contractors and begin a negotiation process in which you decide where you want the price to be and which items can be sacrificed to get it there. The time spent in this phase of the work can be the most valuable (dollars per hour) in the whole job in regard to savings on the project. You and your designer should ers the materials' cost and labor to install all the windows and exterior doors. The work is usually done by the framing contractor.

7. Garage doors: Again, this covers the materials' cost and labor to install the garage doors, openers and related items, usually installed by the framer.

8. Painting: This item covers all painting, interior and exterior, materials and labor performed by a painting contractor.

9. Masonry: This item covers exterior finishes such as stucco, stone or brick veneer and should include labor, masonry materials, and all miscellaneous associated materials, such as steel lintel angles. The work will be done by a plasterer, stone mason or brick mason.

10. Roof: This item covers materials and labor for the finished roof, including underlayment, but not the plywood deck. If there is no section titled "sheet metal work," the roofing line item will include the flashing, gutters and downspouts. This work will be performed by a roofing contractor who may share the sheet metal portion of his contract with a "tinner."

11. Plumbing: This item includes all materials and labor for the plumbing in the yard, slab, walls, floors and roof. The plumbing subcontractor will do the above work in stages, as well as install the plumbing fixtures. The cost of the fixtures themselves will be included in this line item if there is not another line specifically titled "plumbing fixture allowance."

12. A/C and heat: This line item includes the materials and labor for the installation of the air-conditioning and heating systems, including furnaces, blowers, ducts, diffusers. The mechanical subcontractor will perform this work, as well as design the technical aspects of your system. Electrical connections are done by the electrician.

13. Insulation: This covers the materials and labor to install insulation in the walls, floors and ceilings of your house and is performed by an insulation contractor.

14. Electrical: This item covers all materials and labor required to install the electrical system, including hookup (connection at electric meter to utility power), breaker box, disconnects, equipment

wiring, wall outlets, lighting and switches. It also includes wiring for intercom systems, stereos, doorbells, etc. The electrical contractor will perform this work, as well as the installation of switch plates and outlet covers. Specialty wiring, such as alarm systems, telephone or TV cable, may be done by the electrician or by a special installer.

15. Drywall: This item covers materials and labor to install the gypsum board (Sheetrock) interior sheathing or interior wall board. It includes taping, floating, sanding and texturing and is performed by a drywall contractor.

16a. Trim and interior doors: This item includes all wood trim around windows, floors, ceilings, cabinets, etc., as well as the hanging of the interior doors and door trim. It will be performed by a finish carpenter.

16b. Ironwork: This item covers materials and labor to fabricate and install any steel railings, ballasters, ornamental ironwork, steel structural pieces, etc., usually done by a welder and installed in conjunction with a finish carpenter.

17a. Counters: This item covers materials and labor for the installation of all cabinets, shelves, countertops, etc. The cabinetry will be built on site or in a cabinet shop—good quality can be had with either method. Installation will be done by the finish carpenter.

17b. Tilework: This item includes materials and labor for the installation of all ceramic tile (bath walls, floors, shower enclosures, etc.), quarry tiles (kitchen floors, patios), and marble or granite tile (entry foyer). This work will be performed by a tile contractor.

18. Mirrors, glass surrounds: This item covers materials and labor for the installation of specialty glass items, such as bathroom mirrors or glass shower surrounds, and is done by a glazing contractor.

19a. Cleanup: This item covers occasional trash and scrap removal during the job and final cleanup of the finished house and site.

19b. Gradework: This item covers the fill material and the initial grading of the construction pad to remove topsoil and replace with select fill to the desired level. It also includes the finish rough grading of the site when the construction is completed.

20. Floors: This item covers material and labor to install finish floors of various materials, such as wood, vinyl and carpet. Usually, each floor type is installed by a specialty contractor.

21. Light allowance: This is the amount of money in your construction budget to purchase the light fixtures you select. Installation is covered under "electrical."

22. Hardware allowance: This is your budget figure for doorknobs, lock sets, hinges, drawer and cabinet pulls, etc.

23. Appliance allowance: This is your projected budget for all appliances, including refrigerator, washer, dryer, dishwasher, compactor, disposal, ice maker, etc. It does not include mechanical equipment, such as hot water heater or air conditioners, which are under "plumbing" and "A/C and heat" respectively.

24. Addendum: This is an item added to the contract after the total construction price has been agreed to and the contract has been signed. Addenda are extras, not included in the original plans, the cost of which are negotiated and added to the construction price. Whenever possible, it is always better to include everything in the initial construction price before the contract is signed and the contractor is still trying hard to get your job. Once a job is awarded to a particular contractor, extras and additions often have a way of becoming more expensive than they might have been before.

POTENTIAL SAVINGS

Obviously, the higher cost line items offer the largest potential savings, but usually, the fat is spread fairly evenly throughout the total job. Here are some standard places to look for savings.

1. Windows: High quality name brand wood windows can be traded for locally manufactured wood windows or even for painted aluminum windows. Aluminum windows will, however, radically change the appearance of your house. Double glazing (two sheets of glass with an air space) or insulated glass is almost twice the price of single-glazed windows. This extra money is probably well worth it in the northern climates with very cold winters, providing something like a three- to five-year payback on your utility bill. Western and southern areas may have twice as long a payback period, so it may not be worthwhile for the sake of your air-conditioning and heating bill. However, double-glazed windows do not feel "cold" during winter and also block out more noise than single-glazed windows.

2. Countertops: Granite or marble slab or Corian countertops are very expensive. Plastic laminate is a maintenance-free material that comes in countless beautiful colors and patterns. A little creativity in detailing the edges can produce a good-looking countertop and save you much in this area.

3. Interior doors: Nonstandard sizes will cost a good deal more than standard sizes. Slab doors are less expensive than panel doors. Masonite five-panel doors are much less expensive than solid core panel doors and look almost as good.

4. Exterior doors: Again, stick with standard sizes and designs. Sliding glass doors are much cheaper than French doors, and even though the look is entirely different, it is not necessarily a bad look.

5. Glass block: Glass block is very nice and very expensive. Consider sandblasted (frosted) fixed glass panels instead. Again, the look is different, but with a little imagination, it can still be nice.

6. Roof: Any roof other than the standard composition tile roof will come with a great premium, especially concrete tiles, clay tiles, or standing seam metal roofs.

7. Pavers: The price of tile pavers can vary greatly. If you look around, you may be able to find one very similar to your first choice at a greatly reduced price.

8. Insulation: Styrofoam or similar foam insulations are very expensive. Fiberglass batt insulation is the best buy for your insulation dollar, but watch your "R" values. A 2"×4" stud wall can take R-13 or R-15 fiberglass batt insulation, but the extra two units in R-15 come very highly priced. It's probably not worth the money unless your electric company requires it for the "all electric" discount.

9. Wall framing with 2"×6" studs: Many contractors will tell you that using 2"×6" studs in the walls of your house will allow you to put R-19 insulation in your walls. This is true, but since 85 to 90 percent of your heat loss/gain will be through your windows, this extra insulation will not do you much good, and the price of the extra lumber is very high.

10. Carpet: Anything with the word "wool" in it will be very expensive, as will the very heavy carpets (say more than twenty-eight ounces). There are some very handsome commercial carpets on the market in nylon and olefin that will work admirably. Olefin is also very easy to clean and almost impossible to stain.

11. Exterior material: In most locations, brick veneer and stucco are approximately the same price. The cost of the specific brick can vary widely from $150/1,000 bricks to above $400/1,000 bricks. Wood siding will be less expensive, but not the same look and will require more maintenance. Aluminum or vinyl siding may cost less than wood.

12. Large amount line items: It might be worth rebidding some of the large amount line items, such as framing or concrete work. Your contractor has selected a certain subcontractor because he has worked with him before and knows the quality level of the job he is capable of doing. However, another sub may be just as qualified and may be substantially less expensive if he needs the job. Remember, material costs are fairly well set across the industry, but labor and profit can vary greatly depending upon timing.

If you have found a contractor you would like to work with and he is not too far away from your ideal price, tell him where you want the price to be and ask him how you can get it there. He should be glad to sit down with you and go through his bid item by item, making suggestions for potential savings as you go. If no one is close enough for discussion, consider putting the whole job out to bid again to another set of contractors.

Keep in mind that construction is like anything else you purchase: Almost always, a higher quality product will cost you more than one of inferior quality. But of course, there are ways to get better deals if you are familiar with how the market works.

In residential construction, there are many levels of contractor quality. If your bids vary greatly, the reason is probably because of this difference. A better contractor will take more time to understand your plans. He will use better subcontractors, and he will take the time to supervise his subcontractors more closely. He may even use better materials in some areas, such as hard air conditioning duct instead of flexible duct, because he wants to produce a superior product.

Another contractor may have a much lower bid for the same house by using less expensive subcontractors and limiting the time he spends on your project. Because his profit on your house is lower, he will have more homes under construction at one time and will depend on his less experienced subcontractors to supervise themselves.

If your bids are too high with the higher quality builder, you may consider using a less expensive contractor for a large savings and paying a small amount more to your designer to follow the construction. When mistakes are made on your job, your designer can notify you and your contractor, and problems can be corrected before the construction goes too far ahead. And who can better interpret the plans and solve problems than the person who drew them? You may end up paying your designer one or even two thousand dollars more, but you may save twenty thousand on your construction and still receive a quality product.

I often use a less expensive contractor on jobs when the budget is really tight, but I know that I will have to keep a sharp eye on the work. Many mistakes are made, but the contractor is always willing to correct errors when you point them out. I once asked this contractor why he didn't keep a closer tab on his subs so he would not have to always be correcting things. (It seemed to me that it would have to save him money to do it right the first time instead of constantly doing something over.) His explanation was that he could make more money by building more houses at the same time, but it limited the time he could spend on any one house. He felt that it was his subcontractors' responsibility to do their jobs correctly. If something had to be done over, they would just do it and absorb the cost. Of course he was depending on getting by in most cases. Most houses do not have the designer keeping track of the construction, and most mistakes are never noticed by the owner.

This contractor's system usually works for him. But it can also work for you. You can have your designer follow your construction, feel more confident that you are getting the quality you want, and also get the quality at a much reduced price.

CHAPTER ELEVEN REVIEW

Types of bids: A general discussion of the various types of bids and contracts for pricing a project.

Bidding procedure: The correct method to solicit bids from general contractors and sample letters and forms.

Negotiating the price: How to negotiate the closest acceptable bid price to the price you want to pay.

The itemized cost sheet: How to read the general contractor's list of subcontractor labor and materials' prices.

Line items: An explanation of what part of the work is included in each line of the itemized cost sheet.

Potential savings areas: A list of typical places to look for cost savings if your job comes in too high, with explanations of each savings and suggested alternatives.

CHAPTER 12
YOUR CONTRACT AND OTHER LEGAL CONSIDERATIONS

In this chapter, we will cover:

✔ *The standard contract form* ✔ *Other legal considerations*
✔ *Important contract clauses* ✔ *Building codes*

Care must be taken in the preparation of the contract between owner and contractor. Standard forms are available to ensure the clarity and legality of this contract.

STANDARD FORM OF AGREEMENT BETWEEN OWNER AND CONTRACTOR

All contractors will be familiar with some version of the Standard Form of Agreement Between Owner and Contractor. They might have this, or a shorter version called the Abbreviated Agreement Between Owner and Contractor, on their computer and be able to simply fill in the blanks on their CRT and sign it as you wait. This may not be a good idea.

The Standard Form of Agreement Between Owner and Contractor, otherwise known as AIA Document A101, is definitely the form you want to use for your contract. It has been developed by the American Institute of Architects over many years and many judicial opinions. It can be purchased by anyone through the local chapter of the American Institute of Architects for a very small sum (less than $3), and it is worth many times the trouble and price. Even though your contractor may have the same contract in his computer system, it is a good idea to use an original blank form from the AIA since you will know that no important wording or clauses have been modified for "clarification." Your lawyer should be familiar with this contract

form, and if extensive changes are made to the wording, you should have him approve the final form.

The long form is much more complete and detailed than the abbreviated version and should be used for your project unless you are totally trusting in your contractor. Outlined below are important areas of this document that will require your input.

Date of Contract, Place and Parties
The first page lists the date of the contract and the names and addresses of the owner, contractor, and architect, if any, and the project location.

Commencement and Completion of Work
Article Three stipulates the beginning date and duration of the work. Usually, the construction is scheduled to commence within five days of obtaining the building permit.

The date of substantial completion should be inserted in work days or calendar months. During your negotiations, your contractor will tell you when he proposes to complete the job, usually within six to eight months for a medium-sized house.

Most contracts do not have provisions for liquidated damages should the contractor not deliver the work within the required time, so there is really no recourse if the construction time is extended. The completion time is basically a target date, both sides understanding that it is in everyone's best interest to finish as quickly as possible and that the contractor will not be paid his retainage until after substantial completion of the project.

Liquidated damages for failure to deliver the finished project on time may be used in the contract, and a clause stating such may be included in your contract. However, in order to make this clause enforceable, it should be accompanied by some form of reward offered to the contractor if he should finish the project ahead of time.

Contract Sum

The total agreed construction price should be inserted into Article Four as a lump sum, as well as any alternates that have been selected, but were not a part of the original lump sum.

Progress Payments

This section, Article Five, should state when the owner expects to receive the application for payment from the contractor and within what time period the payment will be made, usually ten days after receiving the application each month.

On all commercial and most residential work, the owner pays the contractor 90 percent of the total draw request and withholds the other 10 percent as retainage. This allows the owner to stay ahead of the contractor financially, and the 10 percent retainage guarantees that the contractor does not lose interest in your job before it is completed. Residential contractors always have more to do than they have hours in the day, and they usually need the incentive of retained payment in order to finally get around to those last little items on your punch list. If they still do not perform in a timely manner, there are provisions in the general conditions for the owner to have the work completed himself, and you will need the retainage to cover the cost of the completion.

Article Five should reflect the 10 percent retainage and how that retainage will be ultimately disbursed to the contractor, usually half at substantial completion and the remaining half after the final punch list.

Final Payment

The final payment should not be made until at least ten days after the last punch list is completed and thirty days after you have occupied the house, but never before all signed lien releases and warranties are received from the major subcontractors.

Enumeration of Contract Documents

All documents included in the contract should be listed in Article Nine, along with their dates and the number of pages of each set. Generally it would list the construction documents, the specifications, the soil and foundation report, and any other pertinent documents to the contract like the general conditions, the draw schedule, addenda and alternates.

The draw schedule should list the value of each portion of the work in the approximate order that the work is performed. The total should be the lump sum cost of the construction. This schedule can be prepared on AIA Document G703 and it should be very similar to the contractor's bid form in values and costs. This schedule will be referenced at each progress payment application to ensure that payment applications are in proportion to the already established value of that part of the work.

General Conditions

The General Conditions of the Contract for Construction, AIA Document A201, is a very important accessory to your contract. This document outlines in greater detail the general provisions of the contract and the responsibilities and rights of each party to the contract. It has been approved and endorsed by the Associated General Contractors of America and is the long-established standard form in the industry.

A few of its important clauses are explained below.

Owner's right to carry out the work: This clause states the process by which the owner may correct deficiencies in the work or finish the work himself if the contractor fails to carry out the charge within a certain time. The cost for completing the work, including any extra architectural fees associated with the task, can be deducted from payments due to the contractor.

Review of contract documents and field conditions by the contractor: The contractor is responsible for careful study of the contract documents and is required to report any discrepancies or deficiencies to the architect. The contractor is also required by the general conditions to have studied the site and field conditions and report any potential problems to the architect before commencing the job.

Taxes, permits and fees: The contractor is responsible for paying all taxes and fees and obtaining all permits during the job.

Superintendent: The general conditions require the contractor to employ a competent superintendent who is to be present at the site during the work. Since this can greatly increase the cost of residential construction, it is rarely done. However, even though this clause may be omitted, some understanding should be reached with the contractor before the contract is signed as to how much time he will spend at the site and what his availability to the architect and owner will be.

Samples: The contractor is required to furnish the architect or owner with samples of materials and workmanship by which the work can be judged. Ask your contractor for such samples as marble, granite, wood floors, tile, and any other finish that you want to approve. If the project uses brick, require the contractor to have constructed a sample brick wall (4' × 4' will do) for your approval.

Architect's administration of the contract: If you have a full services contract with your architect, this clause outlines his duties and responsibilities during the construction period.

Claims and disputes: This clause gives a number of steps to be taken toward the settlement of various claims and disputes that may arise during the performance of the contract. A settlement may be simple, such as one based on a decision or ruling by the architect as knowledgeable third party, or the dispute could go through many attempts at resolution, up to and including full arbitration.

Owner's right to perform construction and to award separate contracts: This clause specifies the owner's right to hire his own subcontractor for certain portions of the work and requires the contractor to make room for and cooperate with the outside subcontractor on the site.

Changes in the work: This section deals with the inevitable changes in the work and how they should be handled.

Payments and completion: This section deals with the process of payment application, approval and payments through substantial completion and the final payment.

Insurance and bonds: This section covers in detail all requirements for bonding and insurance for the performance of the work. Many paragraphs in this section will not pertain to residential construction and may be deleted.

Termination and suspension of the contract: This section defines the circumstances by which the contract may be terminated or suspended by the contractor or the owner and the method for doing so.

OTHER LEGAL CONSIDERATIONS

There are a few other legal considerations of which you should be aware even though they may not involve your relationship with your contractor or architect. On any of these items, remember that it is always best to face a potential problem at the onset in the most forthright manner. Most regulatory bodies will work with you to solve a problem if you follow the correct procedures, but no agency will enjoy an attempt to challenge or sidestep its authority.

Special Construction Permits

If your home is to be constructed in a coastal region subject to hurricanes, an earthquake zone or a flood zone, you will probably need to meet some special construction requirements specified by the federal government in order to qualify for the federal insurance protection programs. These requirements are published in construction manuals furnished by the Building Inspection Department in the city or closest county seat.

Official Inspections

If you are building in an area that required you to obtain a building permit, your construction will be monitored by the building officials of that area. Your contractor will make arrangements for them to visit the site during critical times of the construction to inspect the foundation, structure, and electrical, mechanical and plumbing installation. This inspection is required to protect your neighbors from fire hazard and to protect future owners of the property, but it also serves to insure that your contractor is constructing the project in accordance with the approved plans and in a safe and workmanlike manner. These official inspections should not be considered an acceptable alternative to frequent observations by your architect, however, because the city inspector is only observing very specific engineering details with no concern for the aesthetic qualities of your construction.

Rights to Encroach on Easements

Almost every lot will contain utility easements, which may or may not affect the design of your house. Many utility companies will allow specific encroachments into their easements if application is made and approved.

Architectural Control Committee

Most better neighborhoods have certain deed restrictions that apply to each lot in the area and active neighborhood groups that enforce those deed restrictions. Many have Architectural Control Committees that must approve the appearance of any new construction in the neighborhood. This may seem restrictive when you are required to submit, but it will protect your own property values from someone else's bad taste in the future. Generally, these groups are relatively liberal and accepting of any reasonable design. If you anticipate a problem, it might serve to drive around the area before your meeting and make notes of existing properties that have similar features to any you think the Control Committee may find objectionable in your design.

Professional Seals

Many building inspection departments will require an engineer's seal on your foundation plan, but for residential construction, this may be the only legal seal you will need.

The Building Codes

Again, if you are building in a regulated area, you will certainly be required to build according to the provisions of the locally adopted building codes. These codes define the minimum standards for safety in your structure and your plumbing, mechanical and electrical systems and help to keep your design costs down by limiting the necessity for expensive engineering fees on small projects. They also protect you and your family by defining fire and smoke protection devices, fire exiting requirements, and combustion standards for materials.

CHAPTER TWELVE REVIEW

Standard contract form: The suggested standard form for your use for agreement between owner and contractor and instructions on where to obtain it.

Important contract clauses: Explanations of the most important contract clauses.

Other legal considerations: Some other important legal items concerning your construction.

Building codes: A general discussion of building codes and their application and usefulness.

charge or argument. It was an expensive mistake that would have cost only pennies to do right the first time. It was also the kind of mistake that often goes unnoticed for years until the windows begin to rust.

Most residential projects are constructed without the benefit of the designer doing occasional observation, and many mistakes are made that could have been corrected at no expense to the owner or avoided entirely. Most often, the owner is either not made aware of the mistake until much later when the contractor is long gone, or he begrudgingly accepts the mistake because it is too expensive to correct by the time anyone realizes it has been made. Having an occasional inspection by your architect or designer will not prevent mistakes from being made, but should keep the cost of correcting them to a minimum.

The more you have been involved in the project, the more likely you will be able to catch the mistakes. Oftentimes your contractor will not share your concern about how serious a certain problem may be or may not see it as a problem at all.

Without a great deal of construction experience, you will not know how big a problem is either. Even if you are alarmed, it will be difficult to argue the point with your contractor if he thinks it is not important. This is definitely the time to consult your designer for an opinion, and his opinion will usually get the job done right without extra cost to you.

CHAPTER THIRTEEN REVIEW

Critical inspections: The times during construction when a close inspection can be crucial to saving money and time.

Common mistakes: Some common errors made on residential construction and how they can be avoided.

CHAPTER 14

INTERIORS

In this chapter, we will cover:

✔ Some typical interior design fee structures

✔ How to find your interior designer

✔ Types of interior designers

✔ Sample interview questions

Just as you might want the advice of a professional designer when you design your home, you may also want to obtain the services of a professional interior designer when you design your interior finishes.

These professionals are knowledgeable in interior resources such as fabrics, carpets, wallpaper, light fixtures, furniture and sometimes even art. And just as there are many levels of service available for building design, there are a number of types of interior services available and a corresponding assortment of fee structures. These services, in descending fee scale, are as follows:

Interior Design Firm
Independent Interior Designer
Independent Interior Decorator
Interior Specialty Retail Shop
Furniture and/or Fabric Retail Store or Department

TYPICAL INTERIOR DESIGN FEE STRUCTURES

A word about interior fees: There are many basic fee structures in the interior design world, and you should understand and be very clear about the type you select.

Lump Sum Fee

This fee structure is basically the same as for building design and building construction. An agreement is made to perform the service for a certain amount of money. Under this arrangement, the interior designer is expected to pass along 100 percent of his or her discount to the client when the client purchases the fixtures or finishes. Generally, professional discounts (also available to your architect) are from 20 percent (on light fixtures) to 50 percent (on most furniture items). This fee structure is common for most interior design firms and independent interior designers.

This is the most objective and creative interior design assistance because it allows your designer to select from a wider range of suppliers, and since the designer knows in advance that he will be compensated for his time, he can spend more time designing and researching materials.

Percentage of Retail Fee

Under this structure, the interior design consultant works with you for no direct exchange of money, but gets a percentage of the retail price of the items you purchase directly from the retail shop. In this case, the designer may pass along a portion of his own discount to you or no discount at all. It is very difficult for the client to know exactly what kind of price he is actually paying for the item unless he does a great deal of comparative shopping for straight retail prices.

This fee arrangement is used often by interior designers on staff at interior specialty shops and furniture stores and by many interior decorators. Basically, they are like knowledgeable salespeople who get paid on a commission of the sale. Oftentimes, the client will also receive a partial discount on the retail price and feel that he has received free design services as well as a discounted price.

Combination Fee Structure

Some interior designers may ask for a small direct fee for their work and also take a portion of their fee in commission on the sale. This can be a satisfactory arrangement, but it can provide opportunities for overcompensation of the designer without the client's knowledge. If you suspect that this is the situation, ask your architect to verify a few prices of materials for comparison to the prices quoted by your interior designer.

TYPES OF INTERIOR DESIGNERS

The interior design industry does not have a history of regulations and standards for professional status as does the building industry, although some states are beginning to establish those standards. Sometimes the title chosen by the designer may give you some insight into the service he may be providing. The titles and approximate job descriptions in descending level of stature are as follows:

Interior Architect

This title refers to a registered architect who happens to specialize in interior design and space planning. This person is usually involved in commercial interior design and not residential.

Registered Interior Designer

This title refers to an interior designer or architect who has passed an exam administered by the American Society of Interior Designers and has a true professional standing among interior designers.

Interior Designer

This title usually refers to a person with a college degree in interior design and the experience required to do space planning and prepare construction documentation of interior space and details, as well as select colors, materials and furniture.

ASID

If these letters appear behind the name of your designer on his business card, it means that he is a member of the American Society of Interior Designers and probably is among the true professional ranks in the industry. Most of the designers mentioned above will be members of this group.

Interior Decorator

This title usually denotes a professional mainly involved in color selection, material selection, furniture selection, etc. Do not dismiss this person lightly just because he may not have the technical training or experience to produce a document for a building permit. Many of these people are the very best at what they do. Taste and color theory can be learned to some extent in school, but some people seem to have a natural inclination along those lines, and their work is very impressive.

HOW TO FIND YOUR INTERIOR DESIGNER

You can scan the listings in the yellow pages under "Interior Design and Decoration" and get a good idea of the service supplied by the name and listing of the firm.

The American Society of Interior Designers has a free referral service for this purpose. Call them and describe what type of designer you think you want and contact their referrals.

The best way, of course, is to have a personal referral from a friend or colleague who has used a designer who shares your taste. This ideal situation is not always possible, but many of your acquaintances will know someone who is an interior designer you can contact.

Make a list of several selections, call the firm and discuss a few of the following points:

- What kind of interiors work do you specialize in?
- What is your fee structure?
- How much should I expect to pay for what I want?
- What does your service include?
- What kind of purchasing discounts are available to the client?

After a few short conversations, you will be able

to tell which ones are possible candidates. The best possibility might be to call a commercial interior design firm who has no direct interest in your project and ask them to recommend a good residential designer. Their taste may be too avant-garde for your project, but they usually keep up with the best names in the field.

Make a list of candidates, make appointments, and ask to see their portfolios. Try to select someone who specializes in the type of work you want, but most important, try to select someone with whom you feel comfortable and with whom you would like to work closely. Arrogance and intimidation may be good attributes in your maitre d', but they get old fast in your designer.

CHAPTER FOURTEEN REVIEW

Some typical interior design fee structures: Different ways of charging for services and discounting sales of furniture and fixtures.

Types of interior designers: Various types of interior designers and their specialties.

How to find your interior designer: Different ways to locate prospective designers.

Sample interview questions: Some questions to help you find out what you need to know to select your designer.

APPENDIX A: RESPONSIBILITIES CHECKLIST

There are many things to do in order to have a house designed and built. It is difficult to remember all the things that have to be done much less find the time to do them. Many of the items can only be done by individuals, but the responsibility for many others must be shared between different parties, often at different levels of responsibility. Sometimes it is not clear to an owner who is responsible for what.

The following chart lists, in chronological order, the major tasks that must be performed. Beside each item are symbols designating which party has major responsibility for the item and which party has secondary responsibility for completion of the task.

X = Primary Responsibility

O = Secondary Responsibility

Item	Owner	Designer	General Contractor
Evaluate Economics of Building	X	O	O
Arrange for Construction Financing	X		O
Locate and Purchase Site	X		
Gather Design Information	X	O	
Organize Design Program	X	O	
Prepare Schematic Design	O	X	
Price Schematic Design		O	X
Develop Design		X	
Approve Design	X		
Prepare Construction Documents and Specifications		X	
Approve Final Design and Drawings	X		
Prepare Bidding Package	O	X	
Put Job Out for Bid or Negotiation	O	X	
Answer Bid Questions	O	X	
Price Job			X
Obtain Proper Permits, Etc.			X
Obtain Utility Hookups			X
Obtain Insurance			X
Construct Project			X
Answer Questions During Construction	O	X	
Inspect Construction	O	O	X
Review Contractor Pay Requests	O	X	
Make Final Selection of Materials:			
Exterior Finish	X	O	
Paint Colors	X	O	
Carpet	X		
Tile	X		
Countertops	X		
Cabinets	X		
Light Fixtures	X		

Item	Owner	Designer	General Contractor
Door Hardware	X		
Appliances	X		
Plumbing Fixtures	X		
Wallpaper	X		
Arrange Permanent Financing	X		
Make Final Inspection of Job, Write Punch List	O	X	
Complete the Job, Obtain the Certificate of Occupancy			X
Collect Lien Waivers from Subs			X
Collect and Organize Warranties			X
Present Completed Project, Lien Waivers and Warranties to Owner			X

APPENDIX B: CLIENT'S RESIDENCE BID FORM

INSTRUCTIONS TO BIDDERS

1. Obtaining additional prints:
   Write or call Arrow Graphics Company, 3783 Anystreet, Houston, TX 12345; (713) 555-4321.

2. Addenda:
   A. Changes to the documents may be made during the bidding period by written addenda. Refer to plans for sign numbers and to schedule for nomenclature and pertinent details.
   B. Bids are to be based upon addenda issued up to bid time.
   C. Include numbers of addenda received on bid form.

3. Examination of documents and site:
   Bidders are cautioned to carefully examine the bidding documents and the construction site to obtain firsthand knowledge of the conditions affecting the work. Contractors will not be given extra payments for conditions that could be determined or reasonably anticipated in advance by such examination.

4. Notification of document error:
   If a bidder finds discrepancies, ambiguities, omissions or errors of any kind that affect his bid, he is requested to seek immediate clarification or correction. When the bidder turns in his bid, it will be assumed he agrees that any errors that he detected have been appropriately corrected by written addenda or they are of such minor nature that his bid is not affected.

5. Questions:
   A. Questions will be directed to Scott Ballard, telephone (713) 555-1212.
   B. Clarifications, changes and corrections will be made by written addenda to all bidders.
   C. Questions received too late to provide time to inform all bidders will not be answered, so bids will be on the same basis.

6. Substitutions:
   Submit all requests for substitutions as early as possible. If any changes are made, they will be in the form of written addenda.

7. Proposal forms:
   Use only the forms supplied.

8. Bid preparation:
   A. Include all base bid breakdown prices, unit cost items and alternatives in addition to the base bid lump sum.
   B. No varied proposals, segregated bids or assignments will be considered.
   C. Proposals shall be signed with name typed below signature. Where bidder is a corporation, proposals must be signed with the legal name of the corporation, followed by the name of the state of incorporation and the legal signature of an officer authorized to bind the corporation to a contract. If bidder is a partnership, give full names of all partners.

D. Amounts shall be stated in words and figures as arranged for in the form.

E. Submit all bidding documents in a sealed envelope identified with the name of the project and the bidder.

F. Submitted bidding documents are to be originals. Any additional copies may be reproductions.

G. Mailed proposals must be in the hand of the receiver before bid time.

9. Proposal:

The complete proposal consists of the bid form (original plus one copy).

10. Bid evaluation:

Proposals will be evaluated on the basis of the low bid, construction time, of any unit prices and alternates, and other factors the owner wishes to include, such as experience, financial suitability and reputation. The bidder acknowledges the right of the owner to reject any or all bids and to waive any informality or irregularity in any bid received.

11. Bid acceptance:

Bidders agree in submitting a proposal that they will keep the proposal open for acceptance by the owner for forty-five days from bid time.

CLIENT'S RESIDENCE BID FORM

Project: **Architect:**
A New Residence at   Scott Ballard, AIA
1234 Anystreet   1234 West St., Suite 1234
Houston, TX 12345   Towers West
                                      Houston, TX 12345
                                      (713) 555-1212, Fax: 555-1234

To: Mr. & Mrs. Jim Client   _____
    3779 Anystreet
    Houston, TX 12345   (Bidder)
    (713) 555-5678
                              _____

                              (Bidder's Phone Number)

1. Base Bid:

The undersigned agrees to perform the complete work of this project scope (not including alternates) for the lump sum of:

_____ Dollars
(Amount written in words, this governs)

$ _____
(Amount in figures)

2. The undersigned affirms that he has carefully examined the drawings, related documents, specifications and construction site of the project listed above, dated 1 June 19XX, including addenda numbered _____ through _____ inclusive, as prepared by the designer listed above, and has satisfied himself as to all conditions affecting the project.

3. In submitting the bid, the undersigned agrees to:
  A. Hold his bid open for acceptance for the time period specified in the instructions to bidders.
  B. Accept the right of the owner to reject any or all bids, waive any informalities, and accept the bid that the owner considers most advantageous to him.
  C. Enter into and execute a contract, if awarded on the basis of this bid, and furnish performance and payment bonds, at the owner's expense, if requested.
  D. Accomplish the work in accordance with the contract documents.
  E. Complete the work within the contract time.
  F. Accept the provisions of the contract for the owner to withhold 10% of each progress payment as retainage, to be released upon substantial completion of the job.
  G. Furnish financial information as required by owner's potential lenders for loan application.

4. To accompany this bid, and forming part of the complete proposal, are the following documents:
  A. Bidder's experience records
  B. List of subcontractors
  C. Bidder's financial statement

5. Contract Time:
  Bidder hereby agrees to commence work under this contract on or before a date to be specified in a written Notice to Proceed by the owner and to substantially complete the work under this scope within _____ consecutive calendar days thereafter, as agreed between the contractor and the owner.

6. Price Breakdown for Base Bid:
  The clients desire a detailed price breakdown for bid comparisons. The undersigned hereby proposes to perform the following work and supply the following materials for the amounts shown below:

A.	Building pad, piers and foundation	$ _____
B.	Framing	$ _____
C.	Windows, material and labor	$ _____
D.	Insulation and drywall	$ _____
E.	Stucco	$ _____
F.	Roofing and flashing	$ _____
G.	Gutters	$ _____
H.	Millwork	$ _____
I.	Electrical	$ _____
J.	Plumbing	$ _____
K.	Heating and A/C	$ _____
L.	Painting	$ _____
M.	Ceramic tilework	$ _____
N.	Ironworks	$ _____
O.	Allowance items	$ _____
P.	Carpet at $18/sq. yd.	$ _____
Q.	General conditions (permits, insurance, etc.)	$ _____
R.	General contractor fee	$ _____

7. Alternate Prices:
  The undersigned proposes to make the following changes in the construction, including materials

and labor, and if accepted by the owner, to adjust the total bid by the following amounts:

A. Obtain demolition permit, remove all existing structures from site, as well as all concrete foundations and paving. Site is to be totally clean and clear of all debris and ready for new construction to begin. Add: $ _____

B. Substitute clay tile roof for composition shingle roof, such as M.C.A. One-piece "S" mission tile or equal, over 30-pound felt. This price should include respacing roof rafters to sixteen centers. Add: $ _____

C. Substitute wood mantle of the same design for Adoquin stone mantle. Subtract: $ _____

_____
Date

_____   _____
Signature   Signature

_____   _____
Typed Name   Typed Name

_____   _____
Title   Title

APPENDIX C: SAMPLE SPECIFICATIONS

The following pages are representative of a fairly concise set of specifications, which would accompany the sample plan in Chapter Ten. You should check to see that your specifications address the same topics, even if in less detail. In cases of disagreement between owner and contractor, a good set of specifications will usually settle the issue.

A Residence for: Jim and Jenny Client
1234 Anystreet
Houston, TX 12345

SPECIFICATIONS 1 June 19XX

ARTICLES
1. Conditions
2. Excavating and Grading Earth
3. Concrete
4. Stucco
5. Miscellaneous Iron and Steel
6. Sheet Metal Work
7. Carpentry and Millwork
8. Roofing and Insulation
9. Doors and Windows
10. Plaster and Drywall
11. Finishes
12. Painting
13. Electrical
14. Heating, Ventilation and Air-Conditioning
15. Plumbing

1. CONDITIONS

A. Definitions:

1. The contract documents consist of the contract between the owner and the contractor dated _____, the drawings prepared by Scott Ballard, AIA, and specifications, including all written modifications and amendments thereto.

2. The term "owner" shall mean Jim and Jenny Client.

3. The term "contractor" shall mean _____ _____ .

4. The term "architect" shall mean _____ _____ .

5. The term "work" of the contractor includes labor and material, or both, relating to the construction of a residence for the owner at 1234 Anystreet, Houston TX, pursuant to the contract documents.

B. General conditions: The "General Conditions" AIA Document A201, 1987 Edition, as published by the American Institute of Architects, shall become a part of these specifications and shall govern the administration of this contract. Copies may be inspected at the office of the architect.

The contractor is hereby specifically directed, as a condition of this contract, to obtain a copy of Document A201 to acquaint himself with the articles contained therein and to notify and apprise all subcontractors, suppliers, and any other parties to the contract as to its contents.

C. Materials, appliances, employees: Unless otherwise expressly noted herein, the contractor shall provide and pay for all materials, labor, water, tools, equipment, power, etc., necessary for the execution of the work and its completion.

Unless otherwise specified, all material shall be new and all workmanship and materials shall be of the best quality.

D. Permits and regulations: The contractor shall furnish permits necessary for the execution of the work.

E. Protection: The contractor shall provide and maintain adequate protection of all his work from damage and shall protect the owner's property from injury or loss during the period of the execution of the contract. He shall further protect adjoining property, as required by ordinances and these documents.

F. Superintendent: In lieu of a full-time superintendent, the contractor shall be familiar with all drawings and specifications and shall be responsible for the proper coordination and cooperation between the various subcontractors and shall inspect the work each day. The contractor shall be available to the owner for site conferences and explanations on a regular basis or by appointment.

G. Changes in the work: The owner may order changes in the work without invalidating the contract, but any adjustments on the price for such changes shall be agreed to in writing before same is executed.

H. Payments withheld: The owner may withhold payments due, until the objection is remedied, if there is defective work and claims are filed, or there is evidence indicating probable filing of claims.

I. Contractor's liability insurance: The contractor shall maintain such insurance as will protect him from claims under workman's compensation acts and from any other claims for damages for personal injury, including death, that may arise from operations under this contract, whether such operations be by himself or by any subcontractor or anyone directly or indirectly employed by them. Certificates of such insurance shall be filed with the owner and shall be subject to his approval. The general contractor shall indemnify and hold harmless the owner and the owner's architect and engineer for any and all claims of liability arising from property damage, personal injury, etc.

J. Fire insurance: The contractor shall effect and maintain fire insurance upon the whole structure on which the work of this contract is to be done and upon all materials, on or adjacent thereto and intended for use thereon, to at least 80 percent of the value thereof. Any loss is to be made adjustable with and payable to the parties as their interests may appear.

K. Liens: The final payment shall not be made to the contractor until he shall deliver a complete release of all liens arising out of the execution of the contract or receipts in full in lieu thereof. If any liens remain unsatisfied after all payments have been made, the contractor shall refund to the owner all moneys the latter may be compelled to pay out discharging such liens, including all costs and a reasonable attorney's fee.

L. Separate contracts: The owner reserves the right to let other contracts in connection with this work, and the contractor shall afford other contractors reasonable opportunity for the introduction and storage of their materials and the execution of their work.

M. Cleaning up: The contractor shall at all times keep the premises free from accumulation of trash material or rubbish caused by his employees or work. At the completion of the work, he shall remove all his rubbish, tools, scaffolding and the like and shall have the building broom clean.

N. Errors and omissions: If any errors or omissions appear in the drawings, specifications or other contract documents, the contractor shall within ten days after receiving such drawings, specifications or documents notify the owner in writing of such omission or error. In the event of the contractor's failing to give such notice, he will be held responsible for the results of any such errors or omissions and the cost of rectifying the same.

O. Examination of the site: All contractors submitting proposals for this work shall first examine the site and all conditions thereon. All proposals shall take into consideration all such conditions as may affect the work under this contract.

P. Contract time: Upon execution of the contract by the owner, it shall become an obligation of the contractor to complete all work included in this contract within the number of working days he has proposed; the reckoning of such time shall start from the date of the building permit.

Working days shall be deemed not to include Saturdays and Sundays nor legal holidays.

The parties hereto agree that time is of the essence of this contract, and the pecuniary damages would be suffered by the owner if the contractor should not complete all work included in the contract within the number of working days in which he agrees to complete such work, and it is therefore expressly agreed that the contractor shall do everything within his power to finish the work within the agreed time, as extended by any approved extension of time that the contractor shall be granted.

The contractor may be granted extensions of time because of changes ordered in the work or because of strikes, lockouts, fire, unusual delay in transportation, unavoidable casualties, inclement weather, or any causes beyond the contractor's control that the architect shall decide to constitute justifiable delay. The architect shall extend the time for such reasonable times as he may decide subject to the following provisions:

1. No such extensions of time shall be made for delay occurring more than ten (10) days before claim therefore made in writing by the contractor to the architect.

2. In case of continuing cause for delay, only one claim is necessary.

3. Claims for extension of time shall be stated in numbers of whole or half days.

In case of claims for extension of time because of inclement weather, such extensions of time shall be granted only because of inclement weather occurring on normal working days and preventing the execution of major items of work under way at that time.

2. EXCAVATING AND GRADING EARTH

A. The contractor shall do all excavating for foundations and so on required by the drawings. All earth banks shall, when necessary to prevent sliding, be braced against caving inside the working area. The bottoms of all excavations shall be level and all footings shall rest on solid, undisturbed earth.

B. The top twelve inches of earth removed from the site shall be piled separately for the finish grading. All excavated earth in excess of the amount required for finish grading shall be disposed on the site, if required, or removed by the contractor. If additional earth is required for the necessary grading, the contractor shall furnish it.

C. **Grading:** On all sides of the building, the contractor shall bring the finish grades to the lines shown on the drawings. All finish grades shall slope away from the building to the natural grades and finally to the public drainage right-of-way, the topsoil being used for this purpose. There should be no ponding on site.

D. **Clearing site:** The contractor shall remove from the site all obstruction to the progress of the work, including large rocks and old concrete, and the contractor shall protect each noted tree on the site with a 5' × 5' wood barricade. Contractor shall establish the construction entrance for the work.

E. Excavations are to be kept free of standing water at all times.

F. **Repairing present work:** The contractor shall repair and/or replace all pavings, walls, curbs, etc., disturbed during the construction of the building.

G. All structural fill placed at the site shall be placed in maximum 10" loose lifts and compacted to 95 percent standard proctor density at optimum moisture content.

H. **Lines and grades:** The property lines and main floor level will be established by the contractor, and he shall work accurately from these lines and grades.

I. **Capillary drainage:** Fill shall be nonexpansive gravel or crushed stone, ½" to ¾" in size.

J. **Termite control barrier:** Immediately prior to the installation of the polyethylene waterproofing, all areas to receive concrete shall be flooded with an approved chemical treatment approved by the United States Department of Agriculture to prevent termite damage for twenty-five years. A certificate of compliance shall be issued to the owner and the treatment guaranteed for five years. The contractor shall be liable for restoring any damage at his own expense during the guarantee period.

3. CONCRETE

A. All cement used shall be first-class portland cement of an approved brand.

B. Fine aggregate shall be clean, sharp sand, free from loam or other foreign matter.

C. Coarse aggregate shall be hard, clean, washed gravel or approved crushed stone.

D. Any on-site mixing shall be done in an approved batch-machine mixer and shall continue until cement is thoroughly distributed and the mass uniform in color.

E. Forms shall be substantial and unyielding and shall be tight to prevent leakage. Concrete shall not be mixed in freezing weather without taking special precaution to prevent freezing until the concrete has set thoroughly. In excessively hot and dry weather, concrete shall be cured by covering with burlap or other approved material thoroughly saturated with water and maintained moist for a period of seven days.

F. All reinforced concrete shall have a minimum

strength of 3,000 psi at twenty-eight days. Concrete for walks and drives shall be 2,500 psi and water cement ratio of 7:¼. Prepare design mixes for each type and strength of concrete by either laboratory trial batch or field experience methods as specified in ACI 301.

G. The concrete in driveways and walks shall be reinforced with 6 × 6-10/10 welded wire mesh (mesh grid of 6" × 6" and No. 10 bars). Concrete floor slabs shall be reinforced as shown on drawings. All reinforcing steel shall conform to ASTM A615, grade 60 except No. 3 bars that are bent (such as ties and dowels) shall be grade 40. Welded wire fabric shall conform to ASTM A185. Provide PVC sleeves under concrete drives and walks required for installation of future sprinkler system.

H. Concrete forms shall have smooth exterior sides, galvanized anchor bolts, ventilation, plumbing, electrical conduits, pipes, inserts and slab depressions, etc., formed prior to casting of the concrete.

I. Finishes: Floor slabs shall be trowel finished; driveway and walks shall be broom finished. Slab depressions shall be roughened to receive setting mortar. All exposed concrete shall be roughly finished by hand.

4. STUCCO

A. Work required: The contractor shall furnish all items of stucco plaster work shown on the drawings or as specified. All walls shall be built level and true. The contractor shall leave all openings and chases required for mechanical installations.

B. The exterior wall finish shall consist of ½" plywood sheathing with water membrane, galvanized expanded metal lathe, and 2⅜" scratch coats of portland cement stucco. The finish coat shall be an elastomeric coating of a color approved by the owner. Stucco contractor shall consult with the architect for locations of all control joints necessary for the proper application of the material. This wall will extend from grade to the horizontal joint behind the wood cornice at the second floor level.

C. Window frames, door frames, trim, etc.: The wood frames and trim will be finished with an elastomeric finish of a different color than that of the exterior wall.

5. MISCELLANEOUS IRON AND STEEL

A. General: The contractor shall furnish and set all items of structural steel, iron and ornamental members shown on the drawings or hereinafter specified.

B. Painting: All exterior and interior structural ironwork and ornamental ironwork shall have at least two coats of paint in addition to the shop coat. Paint shall be specially prepared, which is recommended by the manufacturers for painting ironwork.

C. Steel lintels: If masonry walls are shown, all openings shall have properly sized galvanized steel lintels, if not otherwise shown. Lintels must be supported by noncombustible structural members, down to the slab below.

D. Steel beams, columns: If structural steel members are shown in the construction, all such items shall conform to the recommendations of the American Institute of Steel Construction and ASTM A36.

E. The contractor shall furnish and install any miscellaneous steel items that shall be required for the proper anchoring and construction of the project, such as column footing, caps, clip angles, joist hangers and stud/plate clips.

6. SHEET METAL WORK

A. General: The contractor shall furnish and install all items of sheet metal work shown or required to protect the building completely.

B. Materials: Galvanized iron shall have an ingot iron base, guaranteed 99 percent pure, and be of a make approved by architect. All solder shall be best grade, one-half tin and one-third lead. Use only resin as flux, with no acids.

C. Flashings: Set flashing and counter flashings of 26-gauge galvanized iron at all intersections of vertical walls and roof, at chimney corners and the like. All flashing to be set with mastic on both sides.

D. Roof valleys: All valleys shall be lined with metal strip extending 8" under roofing on each side, set over 30-pound asphalt felt.

E. Rain gutters: Install 5" painted, galvanized metal gutters on all noted horizontal roof edges, with proper downspouts and anchors.

F. Miscellaneous items: Furnish and install all other items shown on the drawings of 26-gauge metal or better, such as clothes dryer vent, stove hood vent, water heater vents and gas furnace vents.

7. CARPENTRY AND MILLWORK

A. Work required: The contractor shall furnish and erect all woodwork and roofing as shown or indicated on the plans. No finish woodwork is to be put in place or stored in the building until the plastering is finished and thoroughly dry.

B. Dimension lumber: Unless otherwise specified, all dimension lumber shall be No. 2, kiln dried yellow pine or fir. All plates on slab, decking and otherwise exposed lumber shall be wolmanized or equivalent treating to resist rot and mildew. All lumber to be straight and free of defects.

C. Studs: No stud shall be cut more than half its depth to receive piping and ductwork. If more depth is required, the partition studs shall be increased accordingly. Where the running of pipes and ductwork necessitates the cutting of plates, proper provision shall be made for tying together and supporting all structural members affected by such cutting.

D. Roof framing: Frame as per plans. Exterior plywood roof sheathing should be applied with grain of outer plies at right angles to rafters. Plywood shall be of exterior type, no surface or edge shall be exposed to weather. Minimum thickness is to be ½".

E. Exterior walls: All exterior walls shall be wrapped with Dupont Tyvek over ½" exterior grade plywood continuous sheathing. Studs shall be 2" × 4" at 16" on center.

F. Decking: Second level deck shall be 1⅛" plywood decking. Second level decking shall be glued to joist tops and anchored by screws to prevent creaking.

G. Partitions: All studding and partition walls shall be constructed as shown of 2" × 4" studs with plates well spiked 16" on center. Double stud at all openings and all corners unless shown otherwise in plans. Properly truss all openings. Corners for all rooms should be framed solid for interior finish materials. Exterior studs to be 2" × 4" at 16" on cen-

ter. Double bottom plate at second floor.

H. Stairs: Interior stairs are to be as shown on plans, anchored to walls and floors and well supported. Use clear oak treads, painted risers and trim, and ornamental metal handrails.

I. Closets: In all closets the trim and base shall match the adjoining room. Each closet shall have 1" × 12" yellow pine shelves or as specified on plans, pipe hangers of 1" diameter rod. Provide intermediate support for all spans over 4'.

J. Cabinets: Kitchen cabinets shall be constructed of ¾" ash veneer plywood with solid edges and lip molding. Provide clear acrylic finish over natural wood veneer (approved by owner) and at insides of all doors, cabinets, drawers, etc. Kitchen countertops shall be granite slab with full bullnose. All other cabinets, unless otherwise noted on plans, shall be built of wood framing and ¾" birch cabinet plywood with solid exposed edges, lip molding and paint finish. Furnish all cabinets complete as shown on drawings with adjustable shelves and metal drawer guides with nylon rollers at drawers. Cabinet doors to be surface mounted with Stanley wraparound hinges, US 26D finish. All pull handles are to be Stanley wire pulls with brushed stainless steel finish. See plans for countertop materials.

K. Medicine cabinets: Plan calls for wood with louvered door.

L. Wood base: Furnish and install white pine base in all rooms, as shown on drawings.

M. Crown molding: Provide two-piece crown molding throughout first level and at stair foyer at second level. Provide single-piece crown molding throughout the remainder of the second level.

8. ROOFING AND INSULATION

A. Insulation: Furnish and install all insulation in accordance with manufacturer's specifications.
1. Exterior walls—All cracks shall be sealed with Polycel urethane sealer. Exterior sheathing shall be wrapped with Dupont Tyvek House Wrap.
2. Roof—fiberglass batts, Owens-Corning, R-30; Cool-Ply Energy Shield membrane over decking.
3. Walls—4" fiberglass batts, Owens-Corning, R-13.

4. Floors—fiberglass batts, Owens-Corning, R-30.

B. Roofing: Furnish and install mission barrel or S-shaped clay tile roofing as approved by owner. Provide continuous ridge vent at main ridge (only).

9. DOORS AND WINDOWS

A. Weatherstripping: Furnish and install spring bronze weatherstrips complete with interlocking sills for doors.

B. Caulking: All exterior doors and window frames are to be set in masonry and all other intersections of wood and masonry shall be caulked with an approved standard brand of caulking (pure silicon).

C. Door and side light wood frames: The interior parts of the frames exposed shall be made of strictly clear white pine or cypress. Frames are to be completed with blind stop, beads, sills and casing, all as shown on drawings.

D. Windows: All windows shall be as shown on drawings.

1. Operable—Marvin or equal painted wood double-hung window with divided lights and factory screens
2. Fixed—fixed glass to be ¼" plate
3. Glass block—6"×6"×4" PPG (Pittsburgh Plate Glass), Essex pattern

E. Glazing: The contractor shall furnish and set all glass required for doors, windows, side lights, and wherever glass is indicated. All glass shall be properly set with approved material. All window glass shall be double strength. Door and side light glass shall be ¼" plate, tempered. All mirrors shall be copper-backed ¼" plate glass.

F. Wood doors: All doors are to be sandpapered, scraped, and handsmoothed. For size and design, see drawings.

G. Trim: Trim in rooms is to be white pine casing, of a style shown on drawings, at jambs, sills and heads. All interior trim is to be white pine. See detail in plans and provide sample for owner's approval.

H. Rough and finish hardware: Furnish and install all necessary rough hardware, such as nails, wall ties, split rings and builder's hardware to complete the job.

Finish hardware, including locks, butts, door checks and other finish hardware, except as otherwise specified, will be selected by the owner. See hardware schedule for specifics. Contractor will replace, at his own expense, any that is lost or damaged.

10. PLASTER AND DRYWALL

A. Work required: The work to be done under this section includes plastering or drywall finishing of all walls and ceilings as noted on the roof finish schedule.

B. Drywall finish: Areas noted on the schedules and plans to be gypsum board finish shall be faced with ½" gypsum drywall board. Where plasterboard is used, all joints shall be reinforced with tape and putty as specified by the manufacturer; joints and nailheads shall be left smooth for decorating. Walls and ceilings shall be orange peel textured with even finish. Avoid rough textures.

C. Walls and ceiling of the garage area are to be sheathed with an approved one hour fire rated gypsum board. These are to be taped and floated and painted.

D. All wet areas are to be sheathed with water-resistant gypsum board or wonderboard if finished with ceramic tile. Use water-resistant gypsum board if painted. Wet areas are to be taped and floated.

11. FINISHES

A. Carpet: Carpet, where called for in plans, shall be laid over pad over smooth floor and of materials selected by owner. Carpet materials shall be installed according to manufacturer's directions and guaranteed against bulging and moving. The contractor shall include in his bid an allowance of $18/square yard for carpeting materials, pad and installation. Savings in this cost shall revert to the owner, and any extra cost will be borne by him. The contractor shall replace, at his own expense, any that is lost or damaged.

B. Vinyl composition tile: This will be selected by owner.

C. Wood floors: Use ¾″ × 2¼″ standard oak flooring over plywood decking or wood sleepers. Finish with two coats of polyurethane over one coat of stain sealer. Sand between coats with 80-grit screen. Provide owner with samples for selection of stain.

D. Plastic laminate countertops are to be used as selected by owner.

E. Tilework: This section covers the installation of marble and terra-cotta floor tiles, complete. Materials must meet the following standards.

1. Tile—⅜″ thick, 12″ × 12″ stone floor tiles with polished finish and clay tile (quarry tile).
2. Lime—shall conform to ASTM C206 or 207, type S.
3. Portland cement—standard manufacture.
4. Sand for grout—clean, washed, sharp, durable particles free from silt, loam, clay, soluble salts and organic impurities; well graded from coarse to fine.
5. Water—clean and free from impurities.

The floor shall be clean of dirt, dust, oil, grease, etc. Setting beds and tile shall be installed with their respective surfaces to true planes and level, so the surface of the completed flooring will be at the elevation of the finished floor. Joints of the tile shall be spaced according to plan and be straight. The tile shall be cut with a suitable cutting tool, and rough edges shall be rubbed smooth. Tile shall be laid to straight edges, and joints shall be parallel over entire floor.

Upon completion, tile floor and wall surfaces shall be thoroughly cleaned in a manner not to affect the tile surface.

F. Wallpaper: Install as noted in room finish schedule.

G. Ceramic tile: Ceramic tile set on concrete slab may be thin set. Tile set on wood decking must be set in ¾″ mud bed. Baths two and three are to have ceramic toothbrush holders, ceramic tile soap holders with round back, ceramic tile paper dispensers, etc., all to be selected by owner.

H. Showers: Set tile in shower over ¾″ mud bed over lead pan or PVC shower liner. Each shower is to have tiled recess into wall 12″ × 12″ for soap and shampoo shelf. Ceramic tile is to be selected by owner.

12. PAINTING

A. General: The contractor shall furnish material for and execute all painting and varnishing of all exterior woodwork, ironwork, sheet metal in the building, and all interior woodwork, walls, ceilings, etc., as noted in the plans. He shall completely finish and protect the building in accordance with the drawings and the specifications.

B. Character of the work: All finished surfaces shall be left smooth, even, and free from any defects. All brushwork shall show with coating free from brush marks. No paint shall be applied to wet or damp surfaces or before undercoat is dry.

C. Preparation of surfaces: All rust, grease and erection marks shall be removed from surfaces to be painted, and all woodwork shall be sandpapered before starting the work. All nail holes, cracks, etc., shall be puttied full and smooth. Putty shall be applied after the priming coats on surfaces that are to be painted or enameled. Putty shall be tinted to match woodwork on all stained and varnished finishes. All knots, pitch pockets and sap streaks shall be shellacked before paint is applied.

D. Priming: All millwork shall receive prime coats before and after installations. Exterior work shall be primed immediately after erection. When wood siding is used, seal ends before erection.

E. Colors: All colors shall be selected by owner and samples painted for approval before starting the work.

F. Exterior paint: All exterior woodwork shall receive not less than three coats of paint, including the prime coat. Prepared paint furnished by reliable manufacturers specially for this purpose should be used. The prime coat shall be thinned to brushing consistency with thinner recommended by the manufacturer in the case of prepared paint. The second coat and last coat shall be thinned with not more than one pint of recommended thinner to the gallon of paint. Verify selection of paint type with owner.

G. Sheet metal painting: All sheet metal work, except aluminum and zinc, shall be painted before erection with a heavy coat, on both sides, of rust-inhibiting paint and painted after being set in place with two coats of the same material.

H. Interior painting: All surfaces shall be painted with three coats as noted, the first coat in either case to be a sealer type of paint especially manufactured to stop suction. The finish coat shall be either of flat or semigloss prepared paint, used without thinning, as received from the manufacturer. The last coat shall be brush stippled to a uniform finish.

1. Interior drywall:

Step One — first coat polyvinyl acetate primer/sealer

Step Two — texture, light orange peel

Step Three — one coat interior vinyl latex

Step Four — one coat interior vinyl latex

2. Interior woodwork:

Step One — sanding and filling nail holes and caulking with interior latex caulk

Step Two — one coat enamel undercoat

Step Three — enamel semiglow

Step Four — enamel semiglow

3. Finishing interior woodwork:

Step One — stain

Step Two — sanding sealer

Step Three — one coat polyurethane or lacquer

Step Four — puttying nail holes

Step Five — one coat polyurethane semigloss or lacquer

Step Six — one coat polyurethane semigloss or lacquer

13. ELECTRICAL

A. Work required: The installation of all electrical work, including equipment, shall comply with all laws applying to electrical installations in effect in the local community, or with the regulations of the National Electric Code in the absence of such laws, and with the regulations of the electric utility company. After completion of the work, evidence shall be furnished showing compliance with such laws and regulations.

All materials shall be new and shall conform to the standards established by the Underwriters Laboratories, Inc.

All wiring shall be solid copper. The electrical contractor shall calculate the electrical load and size the service as required, minimum 200 amps. The electrical contractor shall furnish, install and coordinate electrical power to HVAC. The electrical contractor shall prewire the house for telephone, cable TV, intercom and stereo. At time of completion, electrical contractor shall test entire system, and system shall be free of all shorts and grounds. All work shall be grounded as required by code. All bath fixtures and outlets shall have ground fault disconnects. Electrical contractor shall verify power requirements of all equipment and appliances to be installed.

Contractor is to notify owner eight weeks in advance as to when electrical wiring is to be complete, so security wiring can be scheduled. Security wiring is to be complete prior to hanging drywall.

Branch circuits' minimum wire size shall be No. 12 gauge. Where the distance from the distribution panel to the outlets is great, or any outlet or series of outlets on a circuit is likely to cause an excessive load, No. 10 gauge wire, or a size adequate for the load to be carried, shall be installed.

All convenience outlets located in the kitchen, dining room and utility room shall be wired with not smaller than No. 12 gauge wire.

Where appliances such as electric ranges, ovens, heaters, air conditioners, or other heavy-duty equipment is to be installed, wire shall be of adequate size for the load to be carried, with no reduction in size between the appliance and the distribution panel and not less than specifications in the following table:

General Lighting Circuits	No. 12	5-15 amp 1 pole
Kitchen Circuits	No. 12	3-20 amp 1 pole
Dishwasher	No. 12	1-20 amp 1 pole
Dryer (if not gas)	No. 10	1-30 amp 2 pole
Clothes Washer	No. 12	1-20 amp 1 pole
Hot Water Heater (if not gas)	No. 10	1-30 amp 2 pole
Bathroom Heaters (if any)	No. 12	2-20 amp 1 pole
Electric Range (if any)	No. 6	1-50 amp 1 pole
Air Conditioner	No. 6	1-70 amp 2 pole

B. Switches: Switches shall be provided where shown. Use rocker-type switches as typical and slide-type dimmer switches where called for, either single-pole, three-way, or four-way, as required. Switches are to be 15-amp, T-rated "silent type." Install at 40" from the floor unless otherwise noted. Dimmers shall be Lutron Electronic for fluorescent or incandescent lighting, as indicated. Size each control to lighting load.

C. Receptacles: All wall receptacles shall be Bryant No. T52-L, or equal, composition body, double-T-slot flush duplex construction, grounded type. Install at 12" from floor or as shown on plans.

All receptacles in bathrooms shall be ground-fault disconnect type.

Floor receptacles, if any, shall be mounted in Lew No. 432 floor box with No. 532-I brass cover plate. Weatherproof receptacles shall be Bryant No. 5352 with No. 868 weatherproof plate.

D. Plates: All switches and wall receptacles shall be covered with plastic standard plates. When switches are grouped, furnish gang plates. Verify color with owner.

E. Panel board/cabinets: Provide central steel panel fuseless automatic circuit breakers, one to each circuit, to provide automatic breaking of the electric circuit when overloads occur. Provide all meter settings, as required by local power company, with neatly hidden 2½" conduit to receive meters.

F. Service connections: Bring in electric service overhead from point shown on plans and approved by local service company. Verify with architect. Provide main breaker in a UL-approved steel cabinet.

G. Fixtures: Fixtures shall be selected or approved by owner. See fixture schedule section for type or budgets. Contractor shall receive, store and install all lighting fixtures, complete with proper lamps, as shown on drawings. Provide all items, brackets, gaskets, etc., required and install according to manufacturers' recommendations.

H. Signal systems: Provide and install approved weatherproof lighted push buttons at entrance doors, electric chimes, transformer, and wiring required for the system.

I. Intercom system: Omit intercom.

J. Telephone system: Contractor shall make arrangements with the telephone company business office for assistance in planning and installing adequate built-in telephone facilities. These will include:

1. Service entrance.
2. Galvanized iron protector cabinet, as required.
3. Standard outlet boxes with telephone jacks and covers at all locations shown on plans.

K. Television outlets: Provide TV cable jack outlets where shown on the drawings. Verify exact locations before installation. Outlet finish and plate are to accommodate owner's TV.

L. Stereo system: Provide stereo wiring and jack outlets from system location to outlet locations shown on plan or verified by owner.

M. Security alarm system: See allowance schedule for budget. Verify locations of keypads with owner.

14. HEATING, VENTILATION AND AIR-CONDITIONING

A. The installation of the heating and air-conditioning system shall comply with all rules and regulations of the National Board of Fire Underwriters and with all applicable local laws and ordinances pertaining thereto. All work shall comply with such regulations, and any such work not conforming to those requirements shall be corrected.

Heating equipment shall be installed in accordance with the manufacturer's instructions except when these instructions conflict with the legal regulations.

All equipment and materials shall be new, standard stock, in sound condition, and shall be installed by experienced workmen familiar with the installation of the type of heating system used.

The heating system shall be a gas-fired furnace central system with two zones (downstairs and upstairs) with 1" insulated fiberglass distribution system. Install room diffusers as shown on plans or as verified by architect on site. Diffuser type and design are to be approved by owner before installation. Consult with architect before final design of system runs and diffuser locations.

B. The HVAC contractor shall size and design the system to the requirements shown below and shall submit shop drawings to the architect for review prior to starting the work. The HVAC system shown on the drawings is for design purposes only as a suggested layout to avoid conflict with lighting and architectural design.

Furnish and install a two-piece direct expansion electric compressor cooling system with an efficiency rating of 12. Locate compressors as shown on plan, with adequate space between. The grand total cooling capacity of the system shall be of a design where the indoor air shall have an entering wet-bulb temperature of sixty-eight degrees Fahrenheit coincident with a ninety-six degree Fahrenheit temperature of the air entering the outdoor unit and 50 percent relative humidity. Unit shall have an SEER of 12 or better, as manufactured by Trane or an equal approved by owner.

The total heating capacity of the system shall be of a design with an indoor temperature of seventy-five degrees Fahrenheit coincident with a twenty-degree Fahrenheit db (dry bulb) temperature of the air outdoors at 85 percent relative humidity. The heating units shall be gas-fired furnaces.

Architect's approval of shop drawings does not constitute the architect's acceptance of the design adequacy of the system. It is the HVAC contractor's responsibility to assure that the system will function properly.

C. All circuits and equipment shall be tested collectively and separately, as may be necessary to determine satisfactory operation. Tests shall include all switching and controls; proper lamping; running of motors; operation of all power, communication and signal equipment; and operation of all appliances and equipment. Adjustments will be made as required for the proper functioning of all items in this work.

15. PLUMBING

A. Scope of work: The specifications and drawings cover furnishing and installing a complete plumbing system as designated and as shown and indicated on the drawings, with such minor details not specifically mentioned or shown as may be necessary to complete the whole system. All work shall be in accordance with local plumbing ordinances and subject to inspection.

B. Sewer and waste piping: Furnish and install all drains and sewers (minimum 4" diameter) to sewer connect. The drainage system above ground, below the slab, and all exterior sanitary and storm sewers shall be Schedule 40 PVC pipe, properly installed over sand and with all the proper fittings.

C. Cleanouts: Furnish and install cleanouts in the house-draining system at the end of each horizontal run, at each branch connection, and at the base of all vertical waste and drainpipes. Cleanouts shall be the same size as pipes they serve.

D. Vents: Provide a complete system of vent risers throughout the building, connecting into waste or sewer line. All vents shall be carried to roofs with proper flashing. No vents may be on north roof facing street.

E. Water supply system: The water service from the city main to the house shall be ¾" minimum. All hot and cold water circulation piping shall be copper tubing, ⅝" minimum. Exposed pipe and fittings used in connection with fixtures shall be chromium-plated brass pipe. No Schedule 40 PVC shall be used under the slab.

F. Hot water supply: Furnish and install, as selected, one water heater in garage with storage tank capacity of not less than sixty gallons. Heater will be gas-fired and properly vented.

G. Fixtures: Furnish and install all plumbing fixtures as indicated. See equipment schedule. All fixtures have been selected by owner prior to installation.

H. Sill cocks: Furnish and install, where indicated, approved sill cocks for exterior.

I. Floor drains: Furnish and install in utility room.

J. Shower: Furnish and install showers, complete, including shower heads with removable faces, adjustable ball joints, seamless brass discharge lines from mixing valves to shower heads with compression supply valves, all as selected by owner. All shower areas shall have water-resistant gypsum board sheathing or equal, finished with ceramic tile, as shown on drawings. See fixture schedule for shower fixtures.

END OF SPECIFICATIONS

Approved by:

Owner _____

Owner _____

Contractor _____

Architect _____

Glossary

Amortization. The liquidation of a debt by regular installment payments.

Blue lines. Reproductions of original construction documents that produce blue lines on a white background.

Blue prints. Outdated system of reproducing original construction documents that produces white lines on a dark blue background.

Builder set. A set of the minimum required construction drawings to obtain a building permit.

Construction documents. The complete set of drawings and written specifications for the construction of a building, being a part of the legal contract for the construction.

Construction loan. The short-term loan that pays for the land, materials and labor required to construct a new building. This loan is funded at the commencing of construction and is usually paid off at the end of the construction period by the permanent mortgage loan.

Cost per square foot. The figure obtained by dividing the total cost of construction (construction contract price) by the area of air-conditioned square feet in the constructed building. This figure does not include cost of land or spaces that are not air-conditioned, such as garages, porches, terraces and decks, but is most often used in comparing construction prices.

Draw request. Monthly request by a contractor to be paid for the materials and labor installed into the project during the previous thirty days, to be drawn from the construction loan.

Equity. That portion of the value of a property left over after deducting the amount still owed on that property.

Escrow. Monies put into the trust of a third party, to be paid to a grantee after certain contractual conditions are met.

General conditions. A general listing of the requirements and understandings upon which a construction contract is based.

Hard costs. All the costs associated with a project that purchase real (hard), resalable components, such as land, building materials or construction labor.

Lien. The right to hold a piece of property of a debtor as security for payment. In construction, subcontractors may file a mechanic's lien on a property if they are not paid for the work they performed on that property.

Massing. The general shapes of the large volumes of the building and their relationship to one another.

Mortgage loan. The long-term loan (fifteen to thirty years) for the financing of a finished project.

Note. A loan agreement.

Program. A written list of requirements to be included in the design of a building.

Punch list. A written list of unfinished or incorrectly finished items that must be finished or corrected before the owner will accept the project from the contractor.

Retainage. The amount (usually 10 percent) held back by an owner out of each payment to the general contractor, to be held as security that the work will be finished and to be paid when the work is complete.

Sepias. Prints of original drawings that are on translucent paper and may be used to make more prints.

Soft costs. All the costs associated with the beginning of a construction project that purchase intangible items that cannot be resold, such as legal fees, architect and engineering fees, loan points and surveys.

Specifications. Written lists, instructions and general information that relate to the construction and make up a part of the total legal contract.

Substantial completion. The time at which the contractor feels that he has essentially finished the project, but before the final inspection and final punch lists are written.

Index

More Books
Packed With Great Ideas

Good Wood Handbook, Second Edition—Now you can select and use the right wood for the job—before you buy. You'll discover valuable information on a wide selection of commercial softwoods and hardwoods—from common uses, color and grain to how the wood glues and takes finish. *#70451/$14.99/128 pages/250 color illus./paperback*

Classic Arts & Crafts Furniture You Can Build—With this guide, even beginning woodworkers will be able to build up to 20 projects—all in the simple, elegant Arts & Crafts style. *#70422/$24.99/128 pages/paperback*

Painting & Decorating Tables—For those special occasions when you want to exercise your creativity and make something special for your home. A master decorative artist shows you how to create special effects, and special looks, for tables of all types—but you can apply the techniques to almost any surface or any object. *#30911/$23.99/112 pages/177 color illus./paperback*

The Complete Guide to Contracting Your Home, 3rd Edition—Learn how your home will be built and where you can save money! This book covers it all, from financing and site selection to working with "subs" and building inspectors. You'll get all the information you need whether you watch from a distance or roll up your sleeves and manage the project! *#70378/$18.99/114 pages/320 b&w illus./paperback*

Build Your Own Entertainment Centers—With three basic designs and four different styles, woodworkers can customize entertainment centers that fit their skill level, tools, style, and budget. *#70354/$22.99/128 pages/229 b&w illus./paperback*

Build Your Dream Home For Less—Save money on every aspect of your home-building—without compromising quality. Licensed general contractor R. Dodge Woodson walks you step-by-step through the building process while explaining how to select subcontractors and materials suppliers, and what work can be easily done yourself. *#70286/$18.99/192 pages/paperback*

The Complete Guide to Log and Cedar Homes—Scores of illustrations lead you through all aspects of purchasing or building your log or cedar home—including all phases of construction. *#70190/$17.99/168 pages/18 illus., 56 photos/paperback*

Creative Window Treatments—Add charm, color and character to your windows using easy-to-follow, step-by-step projects packed with creative and inexpensive uses for fabric in your window treatments. *#70334/$16.99/128 pages/250+ color illus./paperback*

Creative Color Schemes for Your Home—Breathe fresh life into every room of your home with hundreds of creative color treatments. Photographs of successful interiors show you how to create just the right effect. *#70304/$16.99/128 pages/250 color illus./paperback*

Creative Bedroom Decorating—Add charm, color and character to any bedroom—from contemporary, to country, to whimsical—with this vast array of inexpensive and easy-to-do decorating ideas. *#70305/$16.99/128 pages/350 color illus./paperback*

How to Design and Build Your Ideal Woodshop, Revised Edition—This guide features dozens of practical alternatives, tips and solutions for transforming attics, garages, basements or outbuildings into efficient and safe woodshops. *#70522/$27.99/128 pages/paperback*

The Art of the Stonemason—Let a fifth generation stonemason show you how to choose stone; build a wall on sloping ground; create circular walls, window sills, fireplaces, stairs, arches and hunchbacked bridges. Materials needed and techniques to use are covered in detail. *#70005/$17.99/176 pages/133 illus./paperback*

Measure Twice, Cut Once, Revised Edition—Miscalculation will be a thing of the past when you learn these effective techniques for checking and adjusting measuring tools, laying out complex measurements, fixing mistakes, making templates and much more! *#70330/$22.99/144 pages/144 color illus./paperback*

Mortgage Loans: What's Right for You? 4th Edition—Don't make a big-money mistake on the wrong mortgage! Find the facts on what's suited to your financial situation. Plus information on caps, points, margins and more! *#70336/$14.99/144 pages/paperback*

How to Build Classic Garden Furniture—This easy, step-by-step guide will have homeowners, do-it-yourselfers and woodworkers anxious to begin crafting this elegant outdoor furniture. *#70395/$24.99/128 pages/275 color illus./paperback*

Creative Kitchen Decorating—Beautify your kitchen—or create an all-new one—with this recipe book of fabulous design and decorating ideas. Vivid color photographs and clear explanations cover everything from lighting and layout, to storage and work surfaces, plus much more! *#70322/$16.99/128 pages/250+ color illus./paperback*

Creative Wall Decorating—Turn your walls—and your rooms—into masterpieces with this idea-filled book. You'll find exciting examples of innovative techniques, including stenciling, sponge painting, rubber stamping and more. Plus, brilliant color photos and easy-to-follow instructions make your decorating as easy as 1-2-3. *#70317/$16.99/128 pages/250+ color illus./paperback*

Tune Up Your Tools—Bring your tools back to perfect working order and experience safe, accurate cutting, drilling and sanding. With this handy reference you'll discover how to tune up popular woodworking machines, instructions for aligning your tools, troubleshooting charts and many other tips. *#70308/$22.99/144 pages/150 b&w illus./paperback*

Building and Restoring the Hewn Log House—If you yearn for the rustic life, this practical guide will help you build or restore the traditional log cabin. *#70228/$21.99/176 pages/220 b&w, 45 color illus./paperback*

The Weekend Woodworker—Each project provides step-by-step instructions, photographs and diagrams with a comprehensive reference section describing tools, woods and techniques. *#70456/$22.99/144 pages/200 color photographs/paperback*

Creative Living Room Decorating—Breathe fresh life into your living room with hundreds of creative decorating ideas, photographs of successful room settings and displaying tips for getting that sought-after look. *#70318/$16.99/128 pages/250+ color illus./paperback*

100 Keys to Preventing & Fixing Woodworking Mistakes—Stop those mistakes before they happen—and fix those that have already occurred. Numbered tips and color illustrations show you how to work around flaws in wood; fix mistakes made with the saw, plane, router and lathe; repair badly made joints, veneering mishaps and finishing blunders; assemble projects successfully and more! *#70332/$17.99/64 pages/125 color illus.*

Build Your Dream Home for Less— Readers learn how to be their own general contractors and save money on every aspect of home-building—without compromising quality. Walk step-by-step through the building process. *#70286/$18.99/192 pages/paperback*

The Woodworker's Sourcebook, 2nd Edition—Shop for woodworking supplies from home! Self has compiled listings for everything from books and videos to plans and associations. Each listing has an address and telephone number and is rated in terms of quality and price. *#70281/$19.99/ 160 pages/50 illus.*

100 Keys to Woodshop Safety—Make your shop safer than ever with this manual designed to help you avoid potential pitfalls. Tips and illustrations demonstrate the basics of safe shop work—from using electricity safely and avoiding trouble with hand and power tools to ridding your shop of dangerous debris and handling finishing materials. *#70333/$17.99/64 pages/125 color illus.*

The Insider's Guide to Buying Tools— Covers 16 different tool categories, from drills to measuring instruments to high-end production-level equipment to help woodworkers save time and money. *#70473/ $22.99/128 pages/paperback*

Good Wood Routers—Get the most from your router with this comprehensive guide to hand-held power routers and table routing. You'll discover a world of information about types of routers, their uses, maintenance, setup, precision table routing and much, much more. *#70319/$19.99/128 pages/550 color illus.*

Build Your Own Kitchen Cabinets—Superbly detailed, this one-of-a-kind book makes kitchen cabinet-making accessible to woodworkers of all skill levels. *#70376/$22.99/136 pages/170 b&w illus./ paperback*

Woodworker's Guide to Pricing Your Work, Revised Edition—Learn how to set prices and sell their woodworking with this comprehensive guide. Sample business forms and planning sheets ensure prices that are fair and profitable. *#70516/$21.99/ 128 pages/paperback*